趣味識字
Fun with Chinese
A Chinese Character Learning Curriculum

第十冊
Workbook 10

自序

我是一位在美國的自學媽媽,孩子的中文學習完全由我親自教導。

在傳統教學方式的薰陶下許多家長認為孩子學中文必須先從注音開始,往往也認為中文字筆畫眾多複雜對小孩來說太難。其實對幼兒來說每一個中文字都只是一個圖案,幼兒的記憶力非常強,認字對他們來說並不困難。

我自己的兩個孩子都是從認字開始學習中文的。當初我會設計趣味識字是因為在市面上並沒有找到令我完全滿意的教材,絕大多數的教材都是從注音符號或是筆畫簡單的字開始教學。雖然筆劃較少容易書寫但往往這些字在日常生活上並不常見,在孩子的世界裡更是沒有應用的機會。而市面上認字的教材卻普遍地缺乏動手的參與感。孩子在學習的過程中常常覺得教材枯燥乏味,既沒趣味又缺乏實用性。這樣的學習對孩子來說不但痛苦也沒有效率。使用這些教材後我發現自己一直在動手製作輔助教材來提昇孩子的學習興趣。

我一直深信一定要讓孩子覺得有趣和實用,他們才會有學習的動力,有了動力才會學得好。所以趣味識字的設計是以先教常用字的方式讓孩子能夠快速進入閱讀,因而發覺識字的實用性。當孩子懂得如何應用文字後,學習自信自然就提高了。製作輔助教材時為了幫助孩子加強對生字的記憶,除了使用字卡和遊戲的方式複習,我也設計了一系列的遊戲習題,而這些習題就是趣味識字誕生的前奏。

最後非常感謝您選擇趣味識字做為孩子的教材,也希望這套教材可以幫助您的孩子快樂學習中文。

Preface

I am a homeschooling mom in America who successfully taught my two children to read Chinese at a young age.

Many people think that learning Chinese must start with pinyin because Chinese characters are too complicated and believed to be too difficult for children. However, in children's minds, each Chinese character is just like a picture and memorization is not difficult for them.

Both my children learned to read Chinese beginning with character recognition, yet the process was not easy for me. Existing textbooks often start teaching with pinyin or start with rarely used characters with minimal strokes for writing. Books that emphasize character recognition also tend to be less interactive and less hands-on causing the learning process to be tedious and unmotivating for children. I found myself constantly needing to create my own teaching materials while using these textbooks; and this is the reason for the creation of Fun with Chinese.

Fun with Chinese is designed to teach the most commonly used Chinese characters first, quickly allowing children to be able to read meaningful phrases and sentences from the very beginning. Pictures and games are also used to help with character retention, and each lesson includes reading passages to review previously learned characters.

Today, I am sharing with you this wonderful system that I have used with my own children and hoping to make your child's Chinese learning an easy and enjoyable journey.

— Anchia Tai

關於英文翻譯

習題本中的句子都有中英雙語，希望讓中文不是很好的家長們也有辦法使用教材。其中朗讀句子練習中的英文翻譯也盡量讓句型和中文相對應幫助英文為母語的家長容易理解。

About the English Translations

The English translations in the workbooks are specifically designed in a way to closely match up with the Chinese sentence grammar structure. While this might make the translations grammatically incorrect in English, the design will help English speakers to learn and understand the Chinese sentences better.

關於筆順

本書中的國字筆順是依據中華民國教育部「常用國字標準字體筆順學習網」的筆劃順序彙編。中華民國教育部對於部分筆順有做調整，可能於傳統書寫筆順有所差異，不同華人地區的筆順也可能有所不同。如果本書中的筆順與家長所學的筆順有所差異，請自行調整教學。

About the Stroke Orders

The stroke orders of the characters in this workbook follow the stroke orders provided on the "Learning Program for Stroke Order of Frequently Used Chinese Characters" website of the Ministry of Education, R.O.C. (Taiwan). The authors are aware that there were changes to the stroke orders made by the Ministry of Education as well as regional differences in character stroke orders. Please feel free to make adjustments in teaching if the stroke orders are different in your region.

每當完成一課後請回到本頁將該課的愛心塗上顏色。
Please color a heart after you have completed a lesson.

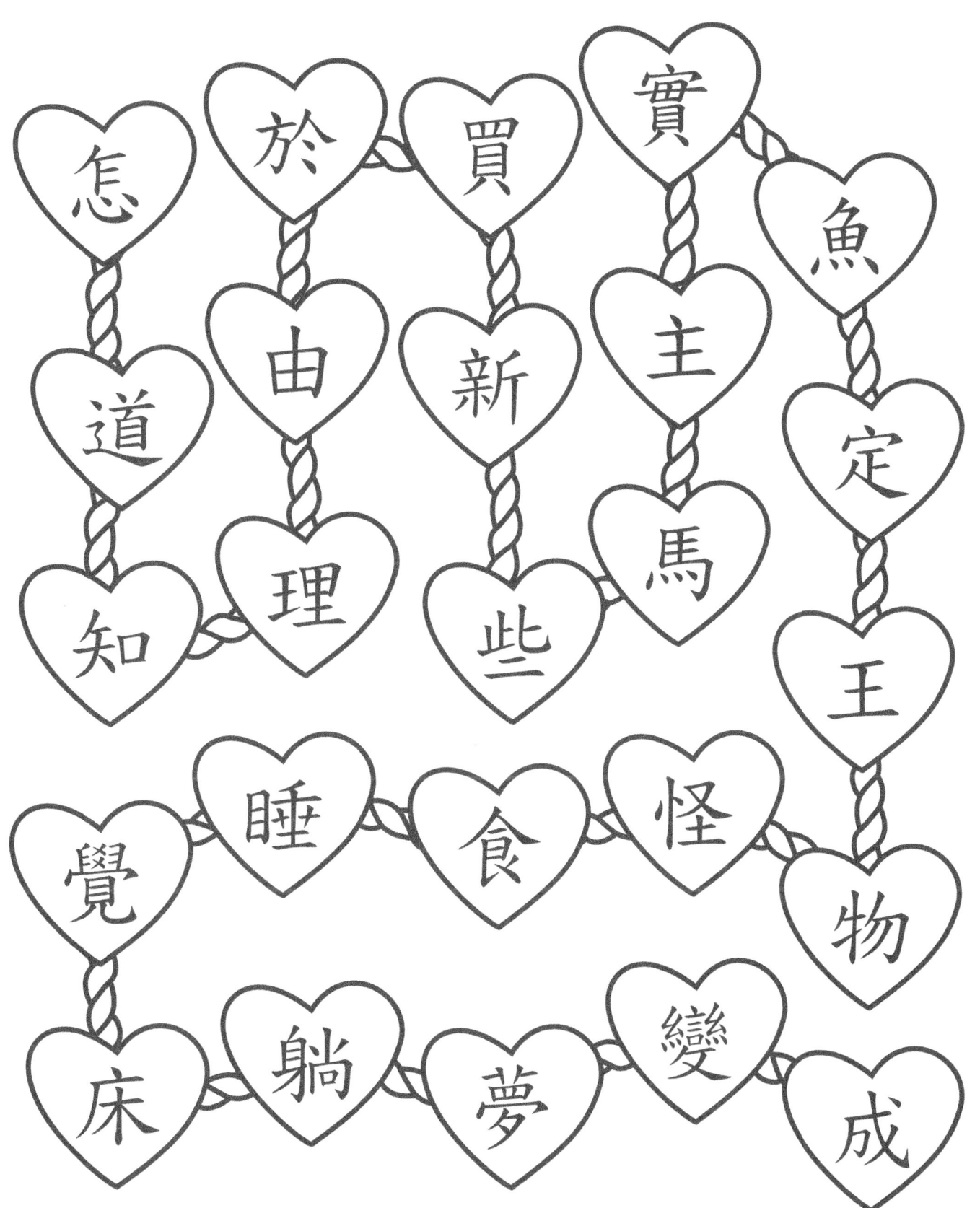

第一課
Lesson 1 Zěn – how

本書中的國字筆順是依據中華民國教育部「常用國字標準字體筆順學習網」的筆劃順序彙編。
The stroke orders of the characters in this workbook follow the stroke orders provided on the "Learning Program for Stroke Order of Frequently Used Chinese Characters" website of the Ministry of Education, R.O.C. (Taiwan).

跟著「怎」字從 ➡ 到 ★ 走出迷宮。
Follow the characters 怎 from the arrow to the star to exit the maze.

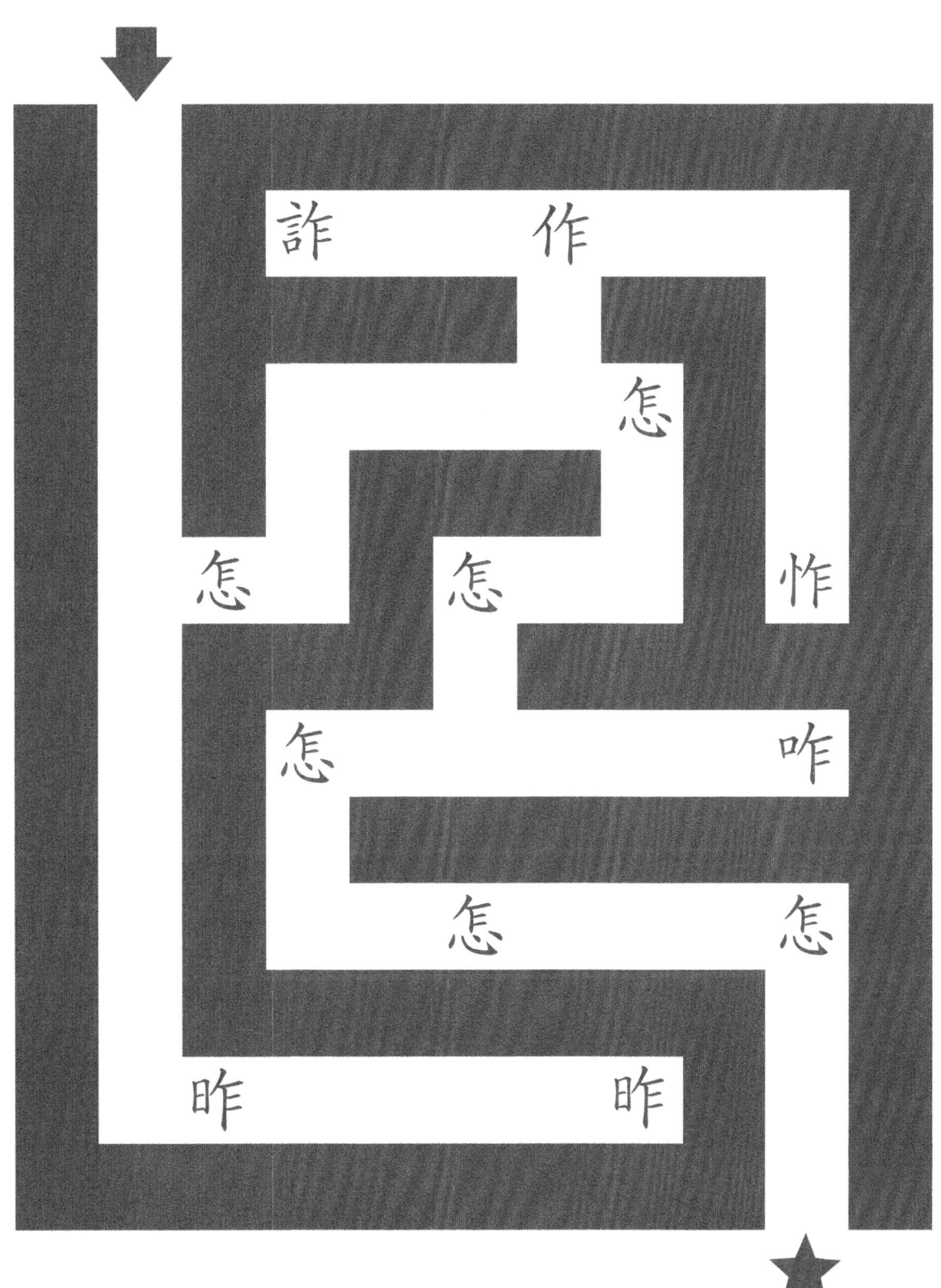

4

請將有「怎」字的地方著色。
Color the areas with the character 怎.

唸唸看
Read-Aloud

- 不得了，發生大事了！
  Oh no! A huge event has happened!

- 我的火雞怎麼不見了？
  Why is my turkey gone?

- 她的現金怎麼也不見了？
  Why is her cash gone as well?

- 我們兩個人都哭得很傷心。
  Both of us cried sadly.

- 會不會是火雞帶著現金跑了？
  Can it be that the turkey took the cash and ran off?

恭喜你完成了這一課，請回到第一頁將本課的愛心塗上顏色。
Congratulations! You have completed a lesson. Please color the heart for this lesson on page 1.

第二課

Lesson 2 Dào – path; reason; to say; principle

本書中的國字筆順是依據中華民國教育部「常用國字標準字體筆順學習網」的筆劃順序彙編。
The stroke orders of the characters in this workbook follow the stroke orders provided on the "Learning Program for Stroke Order of Frequently Used Chinese Characters" website of the Ministry of Education, R.O.C. (Taiwan).

請將有「道」字的地方塗成黑色。
Color the areas with the character 道 black.

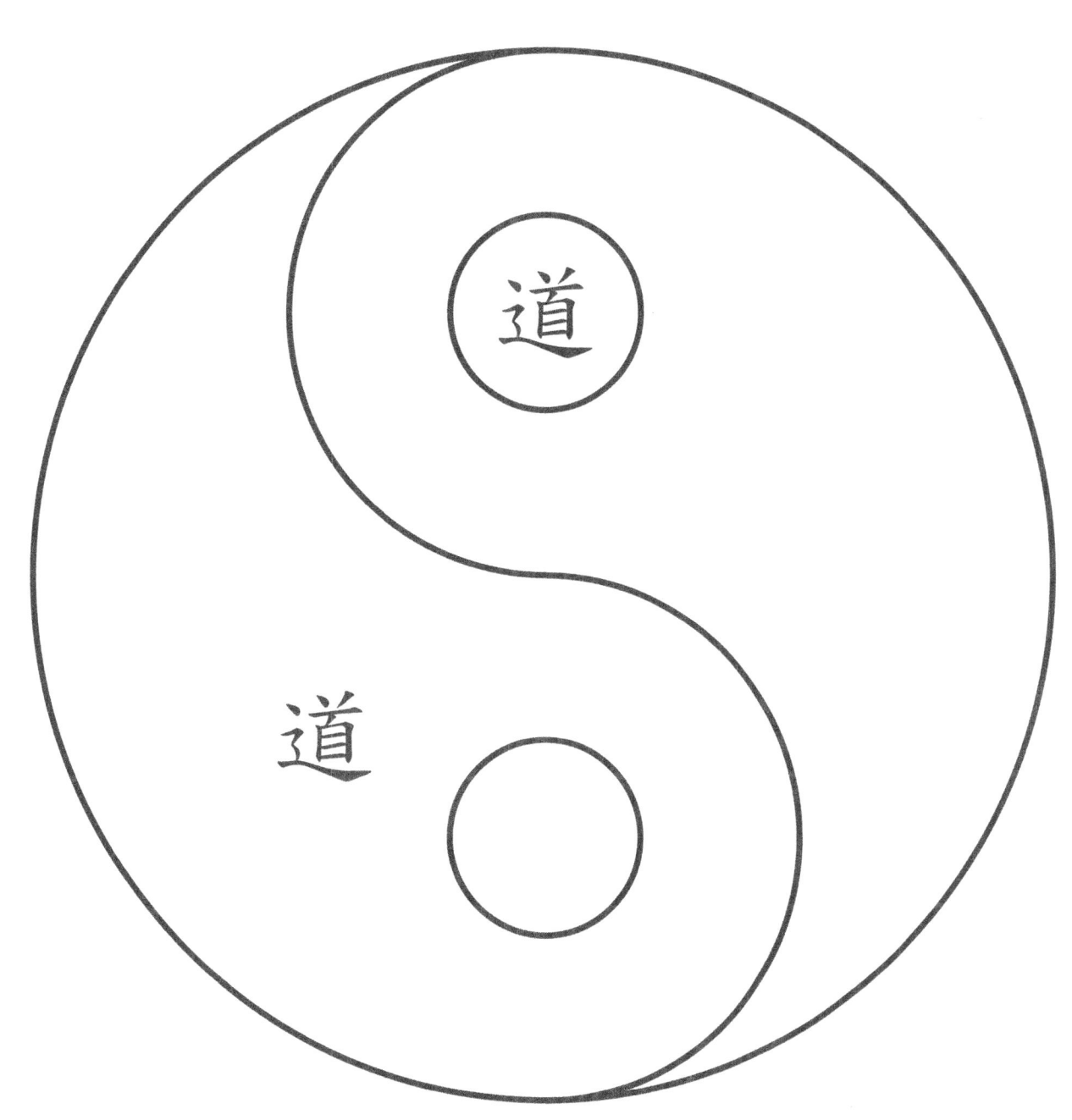

請圈出與圖案相對應的句子。
Please circle the phrase that best describes the picture.

路上有個人。

山上有很多雲。

道路邊有很多樹。

天黑了要回家了。

唸唸看
Read-Aloud

- 爸爸在道路邊看到了現金。
  Dad saw cash on the side of the road.

- 媽媽在道路邊看到了一隻火雞。
  Mom saw a turkey on the side of the road.

- 她問：「火雞怎麼跑出來了？」
  She asked, "How did the turkey ran out?"

- 他問：「這裡為什麼有現金？」
  He asked, "Why is there cash here?"

- 果然是火雞帶著現金跑了。
  The turkey really took the cash and ran.

恭喜你完成了這一課，請回到第一頁將本課的愛心塗上顏色。
Congratulations! You have completed a lesson. Please color the heart for this lesson on page 1.

第三課

Lesson 3 Zhī – to know; to be aware

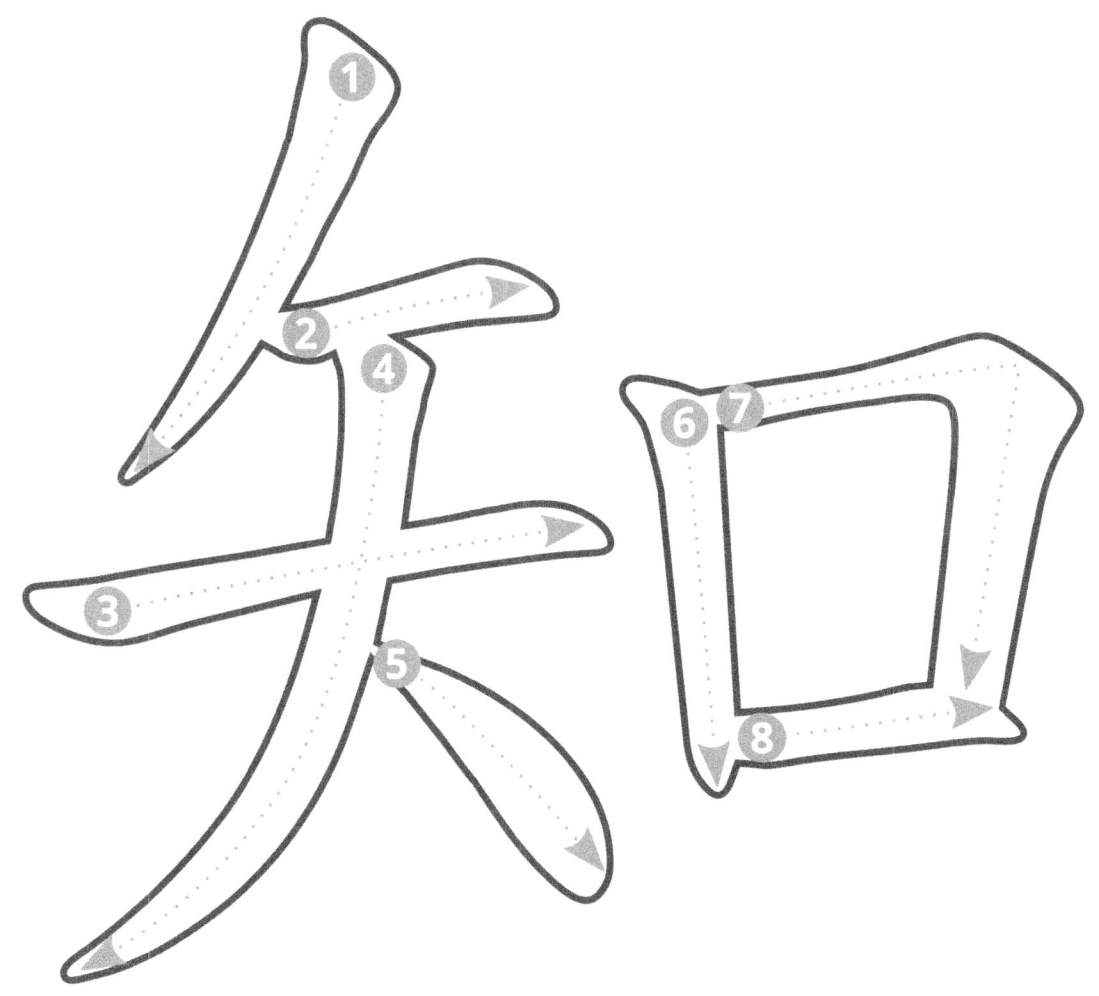

本書中的國字筆順是依據中華民國教育部「常用國字標準字體筆順學習網」的筆劃順序彙編。
The stroke orders of the characters in this workbook follow the stroke orders provided on the "Learning Program for Stroke Order of Frequently Used Chinese Characters" website of the Ministry of Education, R.O.C. (Taiwan).

連連看一樣的字。
Draw a line to the matching character.

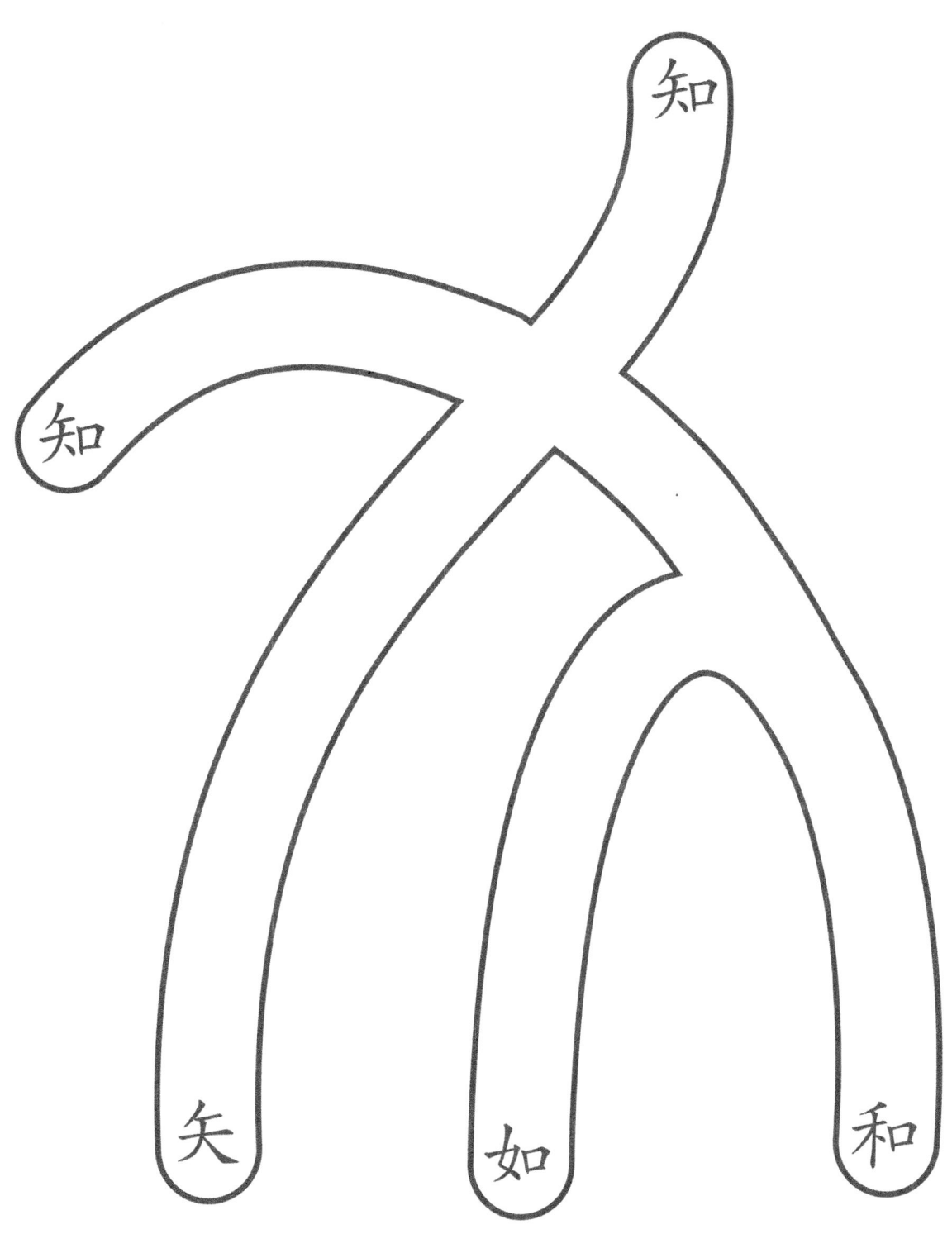

12

找到「知」字圈出來。
Find the characters 知 and circle them.

知　　　　哭

　　　　　金

知　　　　和
　　如

　　道
　　　　知

　　怎
　　　　　她
　　知

唸唸看
Read-Aloud

- 我知道黃金在什麼地方。
  I know where the gold is.

- 你怎麼會知道？
  How do you know?

- 一個老公公和我說的。
  An old man told me.

- 我們一起去看看他說的是不是真的。
  Let's go see if what he says is true or not.

- 那裡只有一隻雞。
  There is only a chicken there.

恭喜你完成了這一課，請回到第一頁將本課的愛心塗上顏色。
Congratulations! You have completed a lesson. Please color the heart for this lesson on page 1.

第四課

Lesson 4 Lǐ – reason; logic; truth; to manage

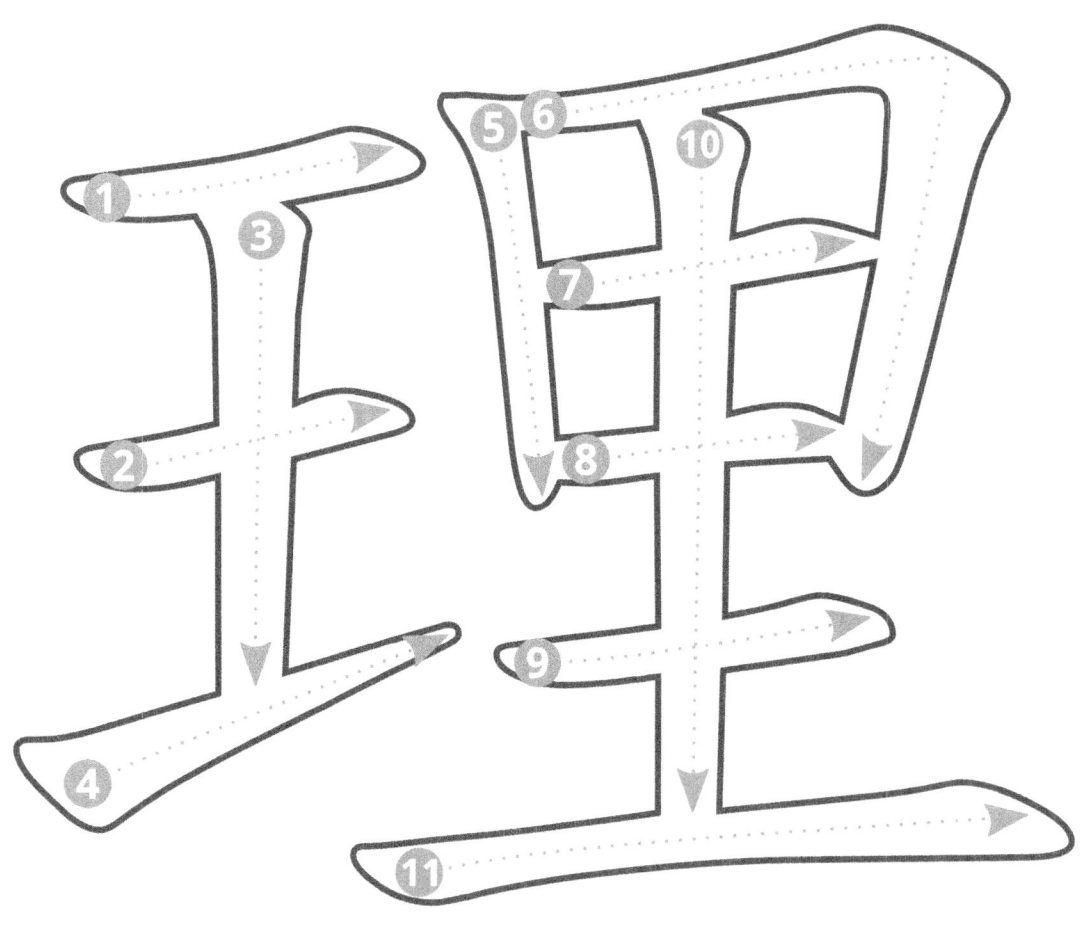

本書中的國字筆順是依據中華民國教育部「常用國字標準字體筆順學習網」的筆劃順序彙編。
The stroke orders of the characters in this workbook follow the stroke orders provided on the "Learning Program for Stroke Order of Frequently Used Chinese Characters" website of the Ministry of Education, R.O.C. (Taiwan).

請將下方的字格剪下來讓孩子選擇正確的字貼上。
Please cut out the characters at the bottom and paste the correct one.

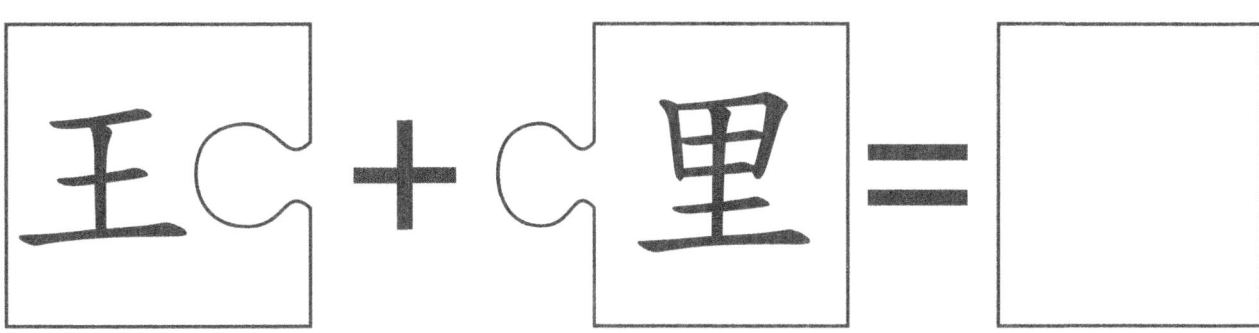

王 裡 理 俚 里

16

將「理」字塗色幫助公主走回城堡。
Color the characters 理 to find the path to the castle.

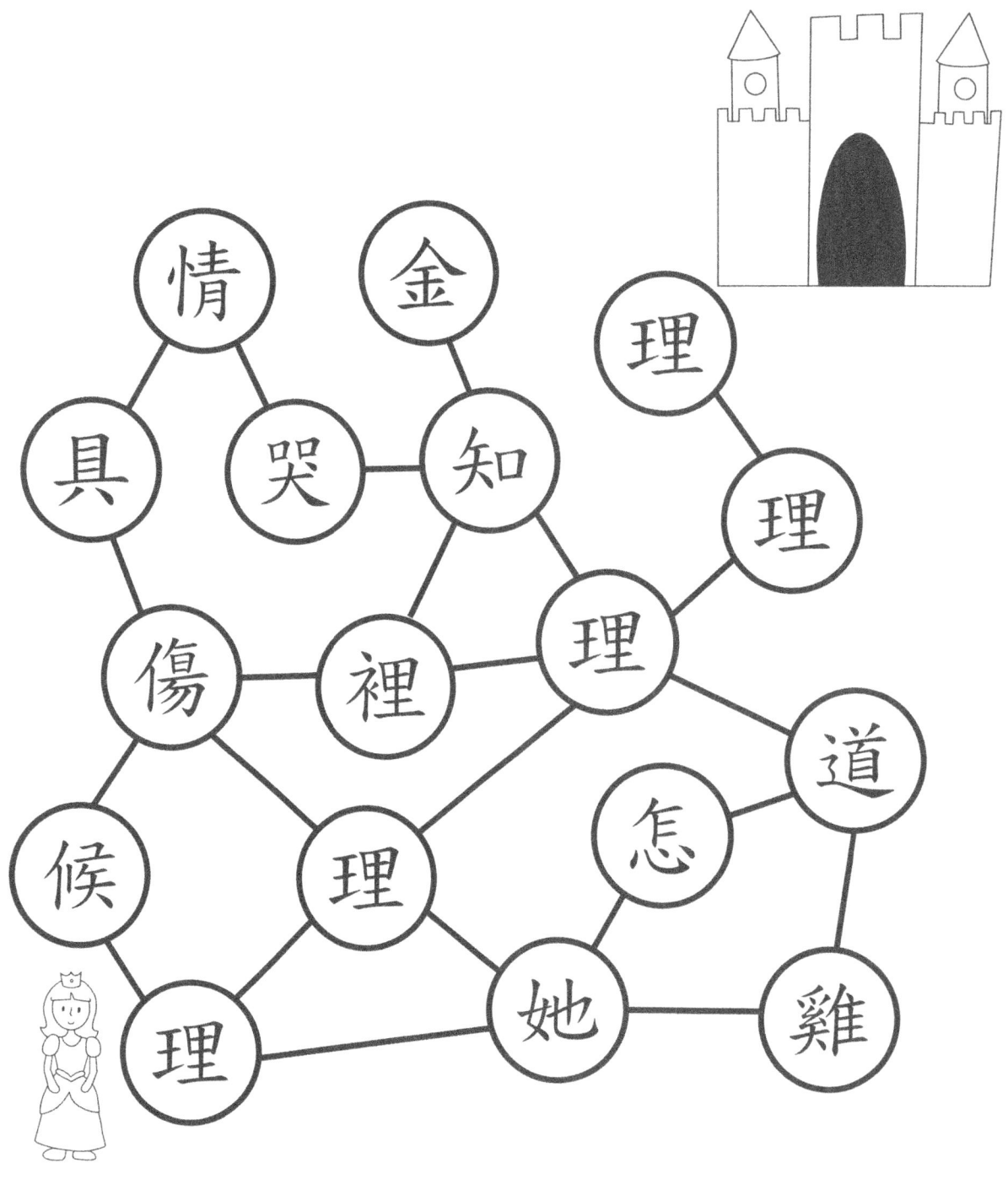

唸唸看
Read-Aloud

- 火雞怎麼可能帶著現金跑？
  How can it be possible that the turkey took the cash and ran?

- 老師說那沒道理。
  The teacher says that does not make sense.

- 我說我不知道。
  I say I don't know.

- 我都是聽小明說的。
  I heard it all from Ming.

- 老師叫我不要理他。
  The teacher tells me to ignore him.

恭喜你完成了這一課，請回到第一頁將本課的愛心塗上顏色。
Congratulations! You have completed a lesson. Please color the heart for this lesson on page 1.

18

第五課

Lesson 5 Yóu – from; due to

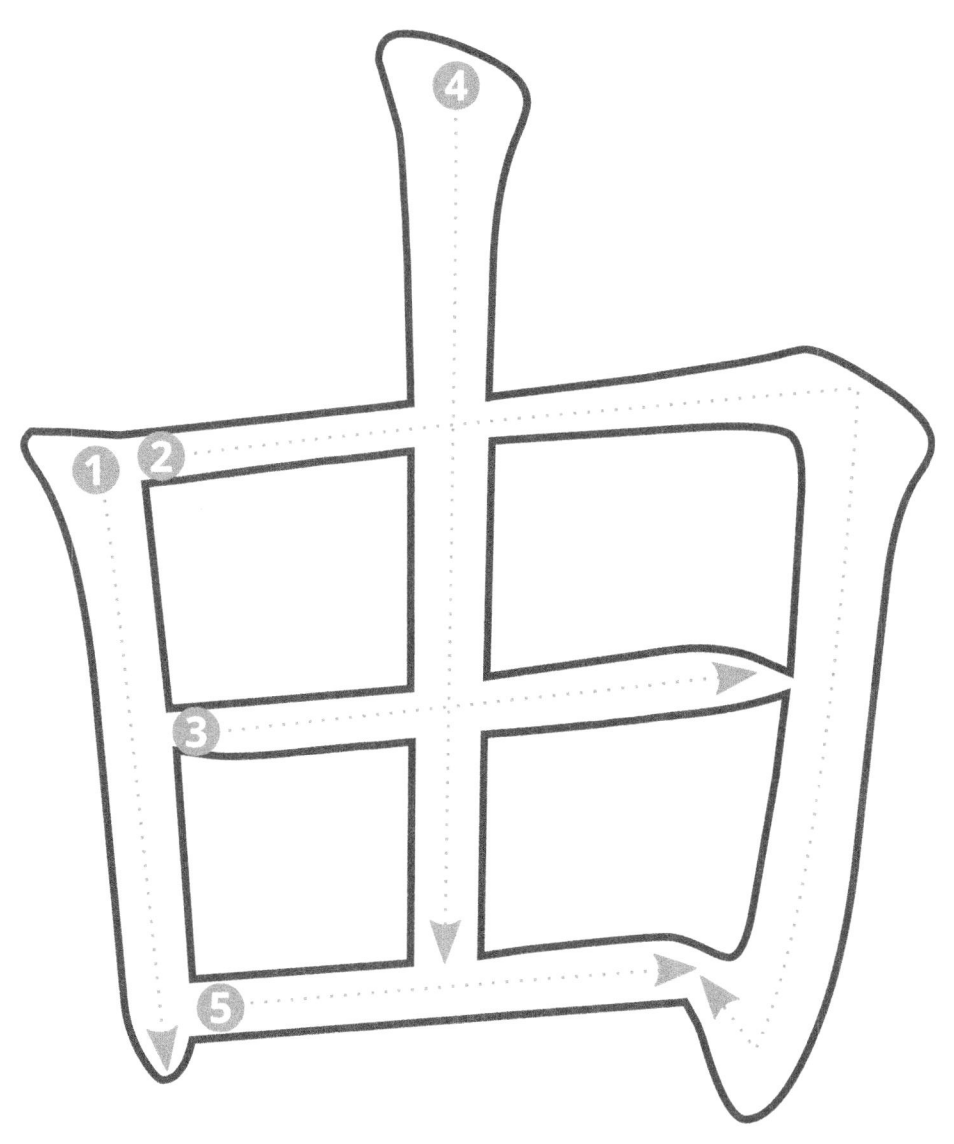

本書中的國字筆順是依據中華民國教育部「常用國字標準字體筆順學習網」的筆劃順序彙編。
The stroke orders of the characters in this workbook follow the stroke orders provided on the "Learning Program for Stroke Order of Frequently Used Chinese Characters" website of the Ministry of Education, R.O.C. (Taiwan).

跟著「由」字從 ➡ 到 ★ 走出迷宮。
Follow the characters 由 from the arrow to the star to exit the maze.

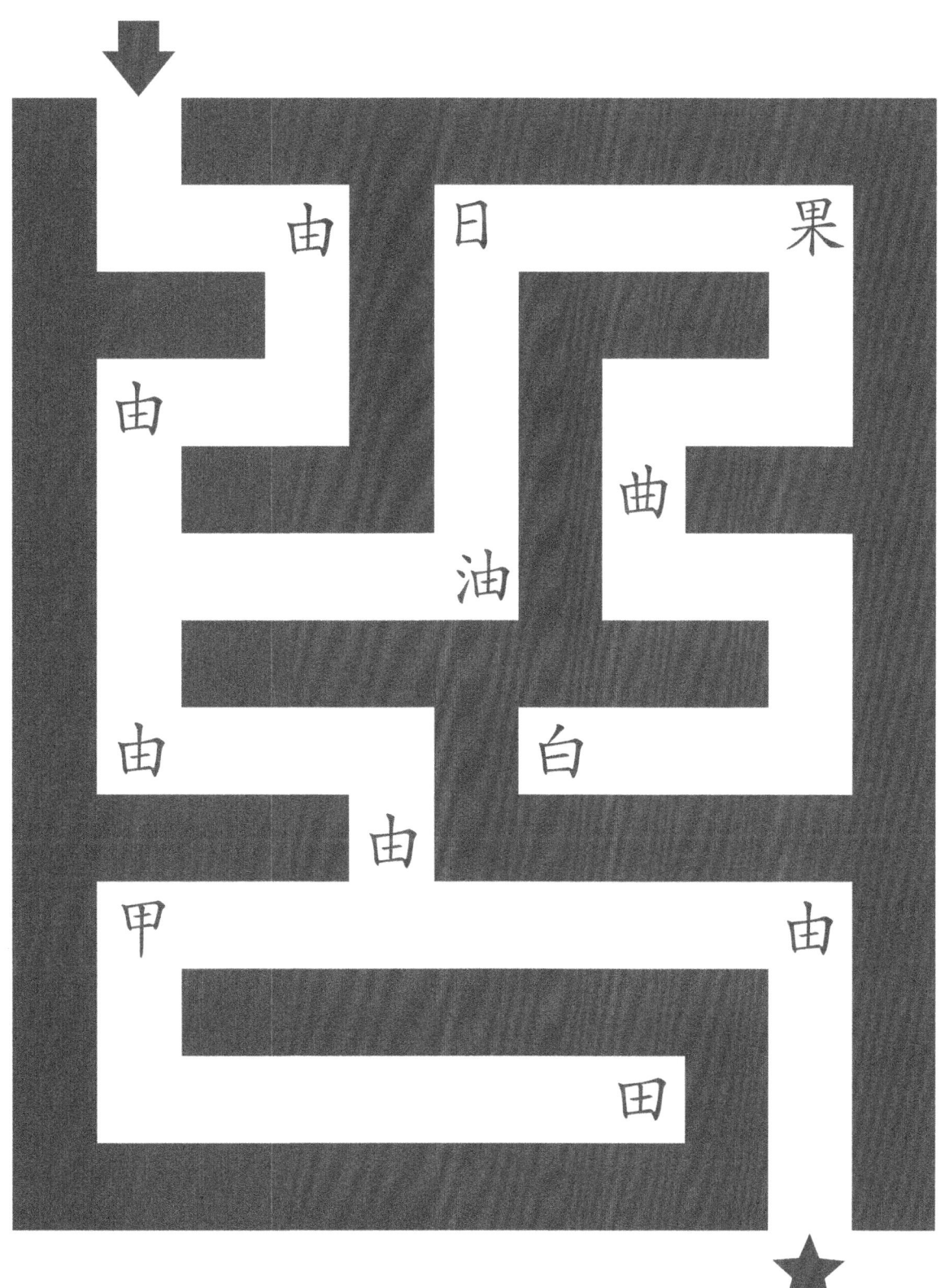

20

找到「由」字圈出來。
Find the characters 由 and circle them.

唸唸看
Read-Aloud

- 我問小明火雞為什麼會帶著現金跑。
I asked Ming why the turkey ran with the cash.

- 他說因為火雞想要自由。
He said it was because the turkey wanted freedom.

- 我說你怎麼知道？
I said how do you know?

- 這是火雞和我說的理由。
This was the reason that the turkey told me.

- 我說火雞不會說話。
I said that turkeys can't talk.

恭喜你完成了這一課，請回到第一頁將本課的愛心塗上顏色。
Congratulations! You have completed a lesson. Please color the heart for this lesson on page 1.

第六課

Lesson 6 Yú – in; at; to; from; by; than; out of

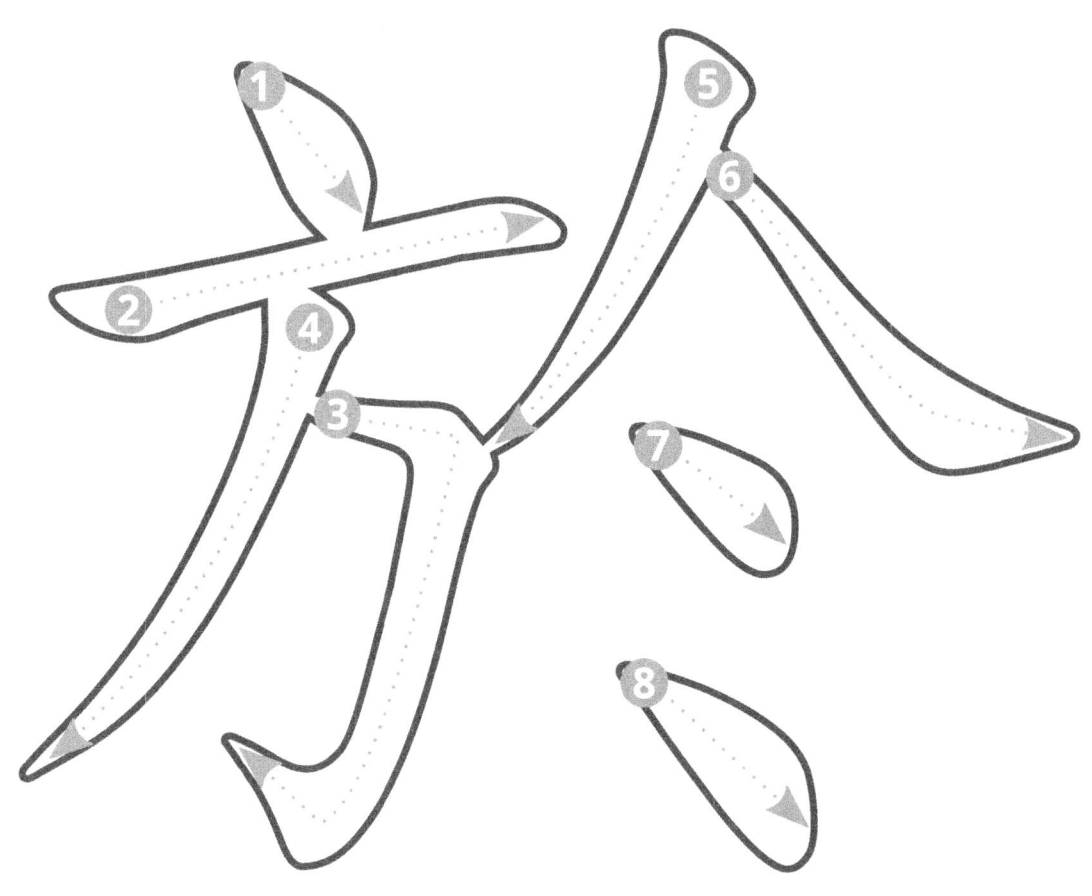

本書中的國字筆順是依據中華民國教育部「常用國字標準字體筆順學習網」的筆劃順序彙編。
The stroke orders of the characters in this workbook follow the stroke orders provided on the "Learning Program for Stroke Order of Frequently Used Chinese Characters" website of the Ministry of Education, R.O.C. (Taiwan).

找出到達「於」字的路。
Find the path leading to the same character.

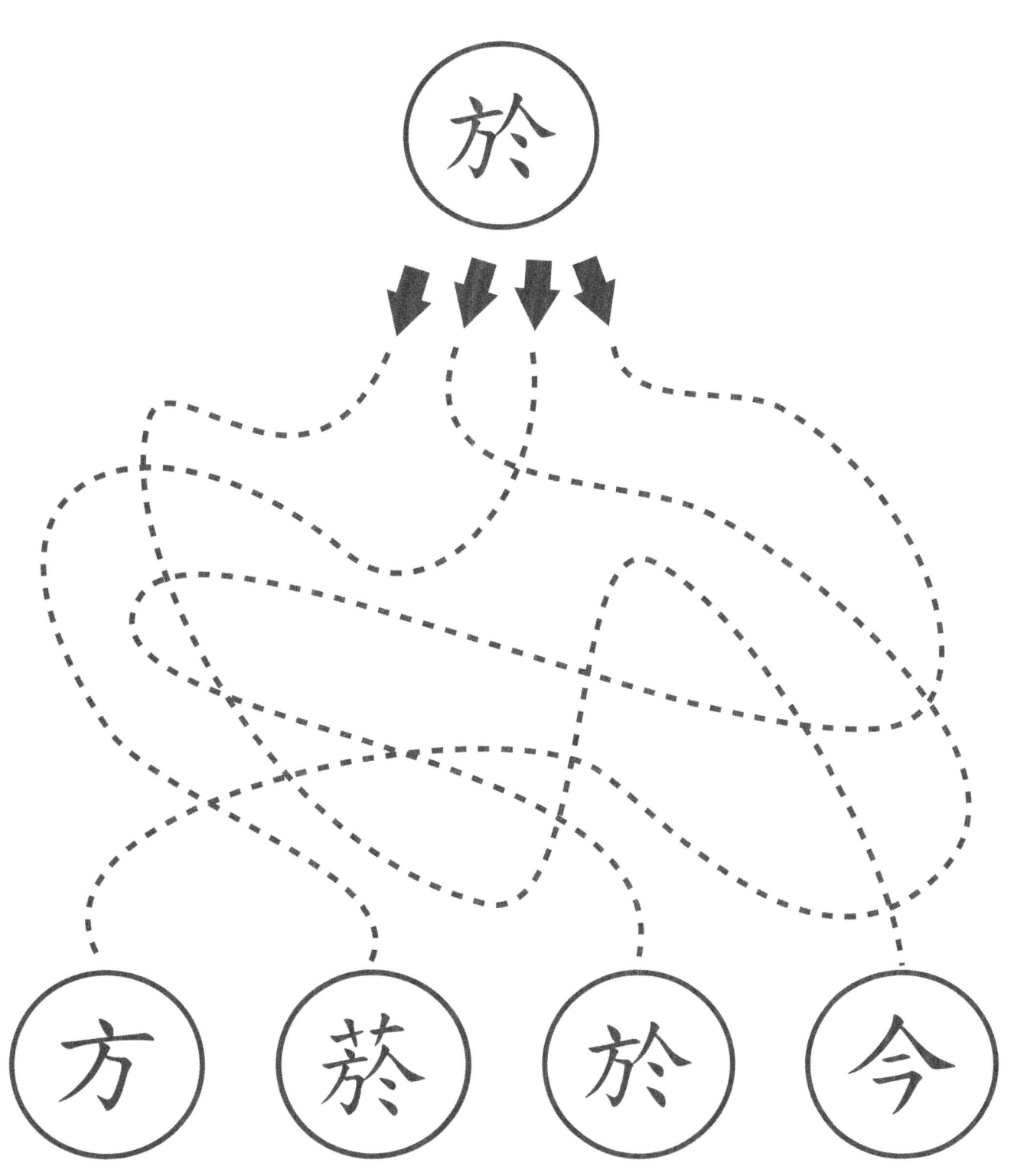

24

請依照下方指示將圖案著色。
Please color the picture according to the following:

於 － 紅色
由 － 藍色
理 － 黃色

唸唸看
Read-Aloud

- 由於弟弟太愛玩，所以沒有把功課寫完。

Because (my) younger brother liked to play too much, therefore, (he) didn't finish (his) homework.

- 老師問他沒寫功課的理由。

The teacher asked him the reason for not finishing homework.

- 於是他說小土狗把他寫好的功課吃了。

Therefore he said that the little mutt ate his finished homework.

- 然後弟弟知道老師生氣了。

Then (my) younger brother knew the teacher was angry.

- 弟弟說：「對不起，下次我會好好用功。」

(My) younger brother said, "Sorry, I will work harder next time."

恭喜你完成了這一課，請回到第一頁將本課的愛心塗上顏色。
Congratulations! You have completed a lesson. Please color the heart for this lesson on page 1.

第七課

Lesson 7 Mǎi – to buy; to purchase

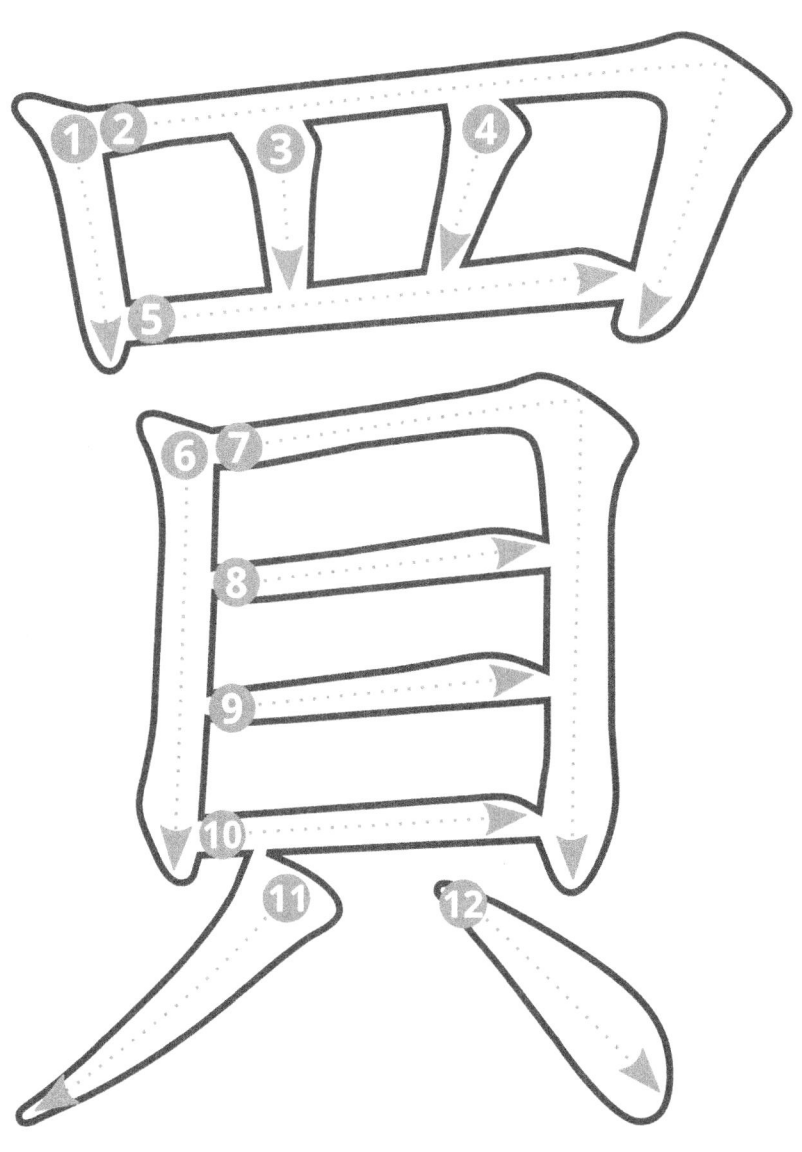

本書中的國字筆順是依據中華民國教育部「常用國字標準字體筆順學習網」的筆劃順序彙編。
The stroke orders of the characters in this workbook follow the stroke orders provided on the "Learning Program for Stroke Order of Frequently Used Chinese Characters" website of the Ministry of Education, R.O.C. (Taiwan).

請圈出與圖案相對應的句子。
Please circle the phrase that best describes the picture.

她正在吃東西。
她買了很多東西。
那邊有隻小黃狗。

將「買」字連到可購買的物品上。
Connect the character 買 to items that can be bought.

- 車子
- 心情

買
- 才能

- 書本
- 氣球

唸唸看
Read-Aloud

- 老師問媽媽知不知道妹妹沒有做功課的理由是什麼。

  The teacher asked Mom if she knew why my younger sister didn't do (her) homework.

- 於是媽媽說:「我買了一個玩具給她,她玩了一個晚上。」

  Therefore Mom said, "I bought a toy for her, and she played the whole night."

- 媽媽回家和妹妹說:「寫完功課才可以玩玩具,不然下次就不買玩具給你了。」

  Mom went home and told (my) younger sister, "(You) can only play with toys after finishing homework, otherwise (I) will not buy toys for you next time."

恭喜你完成了這一課,請回到第一頁將本課的愛心塗上顏色。
Congratulations! You have completed a lesson. Please color the heart for this lesson on page 1.

第八課

Lesson 8 Xīn – new

本書中的國字筆順是依據中華民國教育部「常用國字標準字體筆順學習網」的筆劃順序彙編。
The stroke orders of the characters in this workbook follow the stroke orders provided on the "Learning Program for Stroke Order of Frequently Used Chinese Characters" website of the Ministry of Education, R.O.C. (Taiwan).

31

請圈出與文字相對應的圖案。
Please circle the pictures that best match the characters in front.

新

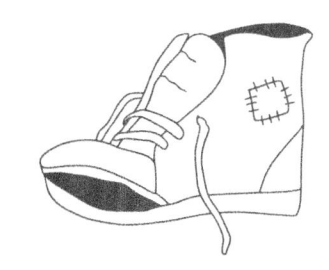

高

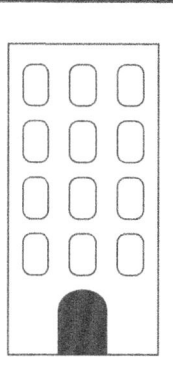

老

大

請圈出與圖案相對應的句子。
Please circle the phrase that best describes the picture.

門口有兩隻雞。

我們的新家很大。

我在路上看到羊。

爸爸正在工作。

唸唸看
Read-Aloud

- 今天天氣很好，天空中有幾朵白雲。
  The weather is very good today. There are some white clouds in the sky.

- 哥哥的心情也很好。
  (My) elder brother's mood is also very good.

- 於是他帶著新買的中文書走到公園裡。
  Therefore he brings his newly bought Chinese book to the park.

- 他從書本中學會了很多新道理。
  He learns a lot of new knowledge from the book.

- 他回來和我說故事的由來。
  He comes back and tells me the origin of stories.

恭喜你完成了這一課，請回到第一頁將本課的愛心塗上顏色。
Congratulations! You have completed a lesson. Please color the heart for this lesson on page 1.

第九課

Lesson 9 Xiē – some; a few; several

本書中的國字筆順是依據中華民國教育部「常用國字標準字體筆順學習網」的筆劃順序彙編。
The stroke orders of the characters in this workbook follow the stroke orders provided on the "Learning Program for Stroke Order of Frequently Used Chinese Characters" website of the Ministry of Education, R.O.C. (Taiwan).

請圈出與圖案相對應的句子。
Please circle the phrase that best describes the picture.

這些人正在開會。

大家在唱歌。

媽媽很愛我。

36

跟著「些」字從 ➡ 到 ★ 走出迷宮。
Follow the characters 些 from the arrow to the star to exit the maze.

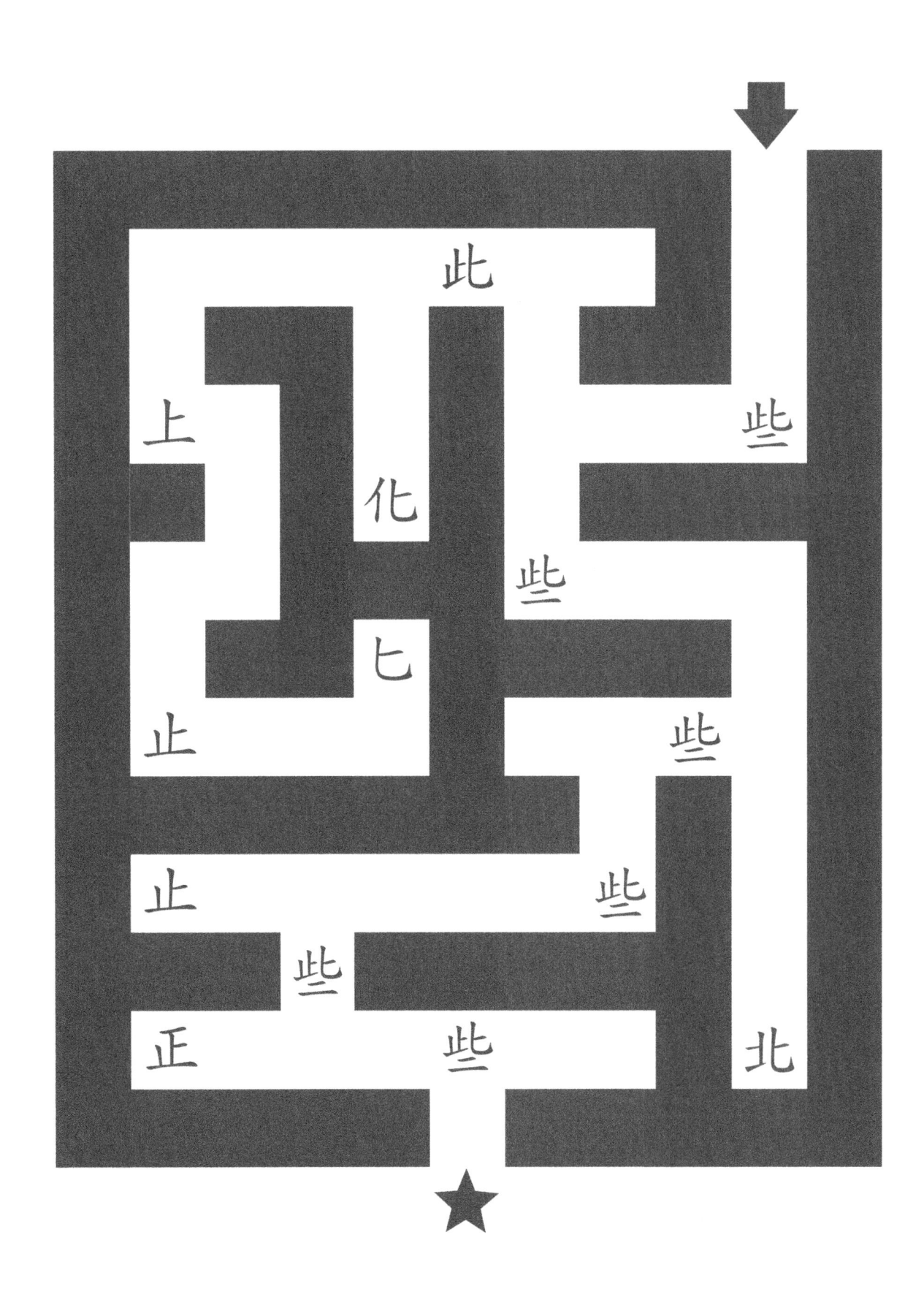

唸唸看
Read-Aloud

- 過新年的時候奶奶買了一些花。
  During the New Year's, Grandma bought some flowers.

- 有紅色的、黃色的，還有藍色的。
  There were red ones, yellow ones, and also blue ones.

- 由於怕兔子會吃花，奶奶也買了一些草。
  Because (she) was afraid that the rabbit would eat the flowers, Grandma also bought some grass.

- 兔子看見草很開心。
  The rabbit was happy to see the grass.

- 奶奶問我：「花朵美麗嗎？」
  Grandma asked me, "Are the flowers beautiful?"

恭喜你完成了這一課，請回到第一頁將本課的愛心塗上顏色。
Congratulations! You have completed a lesson. Please color the heart for this lesson on page 1.

第十課

Lesson 10 Mǎ – horse

本書中的國字筆順是依據中華民國教育部「常用國字標準字體筆順學習網」的筆劃順序彙編。
The stroke orders of the characters in this workbook follow the stroke orders provided on the "Learning Program for Stroke Order of Frequently Used Chinese Characters" website of the Ministry of Education, R.O.C. (Taiwan).

「馬」是象形字，它看起來就像一匹馬的樣子。
The character 馬 is a pictograph. It looks like a horse.

40

連連看
Connect the characters to the correct pictures.

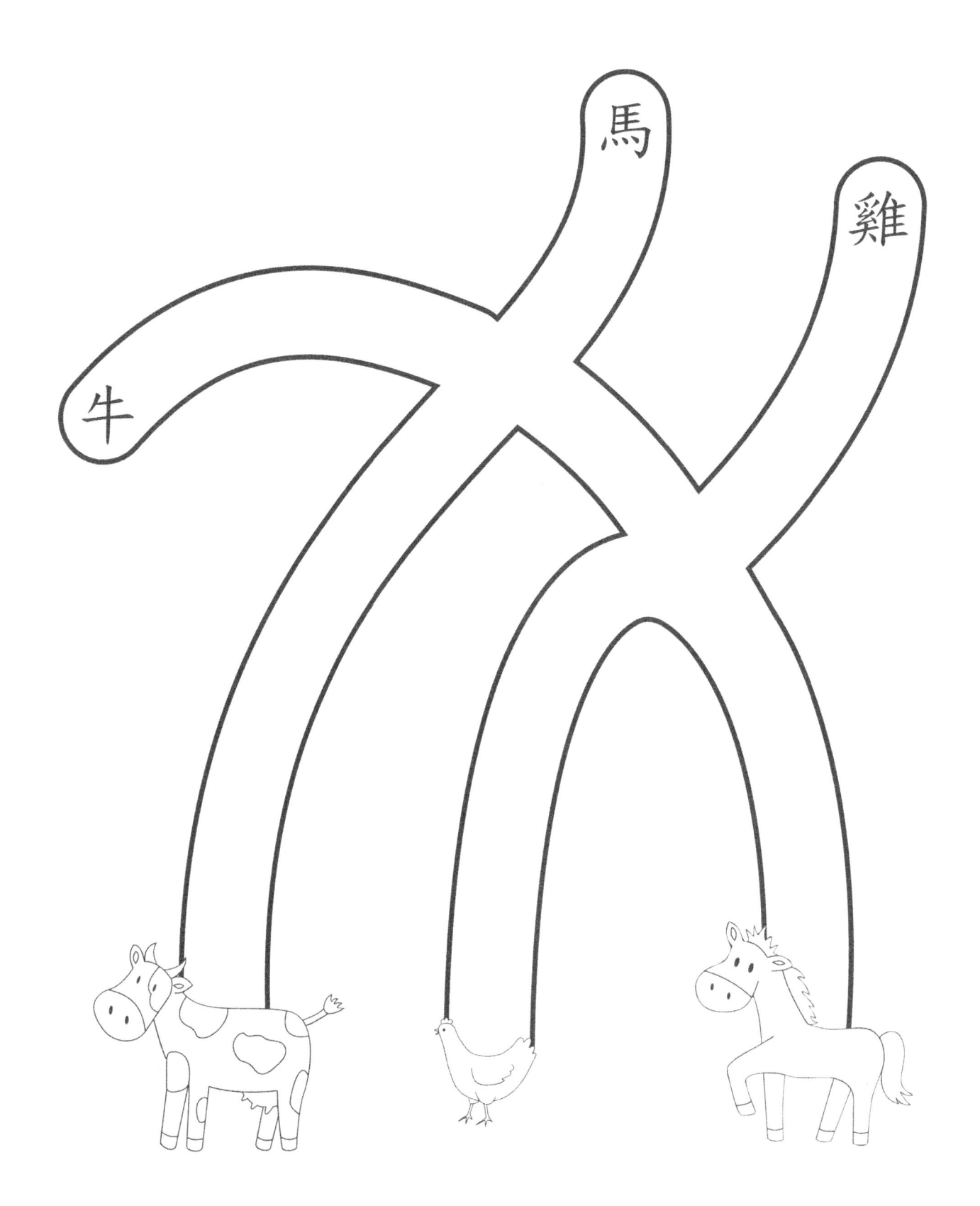

唸唸看
Read-Aloud

- 綠地上有牛、有羊、有馬,還有一些又高又大的樹。
  On the green field, there are cows, sheep, horses, and some tall and big trees.

- 馬兒吃了一些草就跑了。
  The horse ate some grass and ran off.

- 然後羊把最後的草也吃了。
  Then the sheep ate the last grass.

- 於是我只好買一些新的草回來。
  Therefore I can only buy some new grass back.

恭喜你完成了這一課,請回到第一頁將本課的愛心塗上顏色。
Congratulations! You have completed a lesson. Please color the heart for this lesson on page 1.

第十一課

Lesson 11 Zhǔ – owner; master; host; main

本書中的國字筆順是依據中華民國教育部「常用國字標準字體筆順學習網」的筆劃順序彙編。
The stroke orders of the characters in this workbook follow the stroke orders provided on the "Learning Program for Stroke Order of Frequently Used Chinese Characters" website of the Ministry of Education, R.O.C. (Taiwan).

請圈出與圖案相對應的句子。
Please circle the phrase that best describes the picture.

狗的主人不見了。

狗主人帶著小狗一起走路。

狗主人帶著一隻貓。

小狗不見了。

找出「主」字圈出來。
Find the characters 主 and circle them.

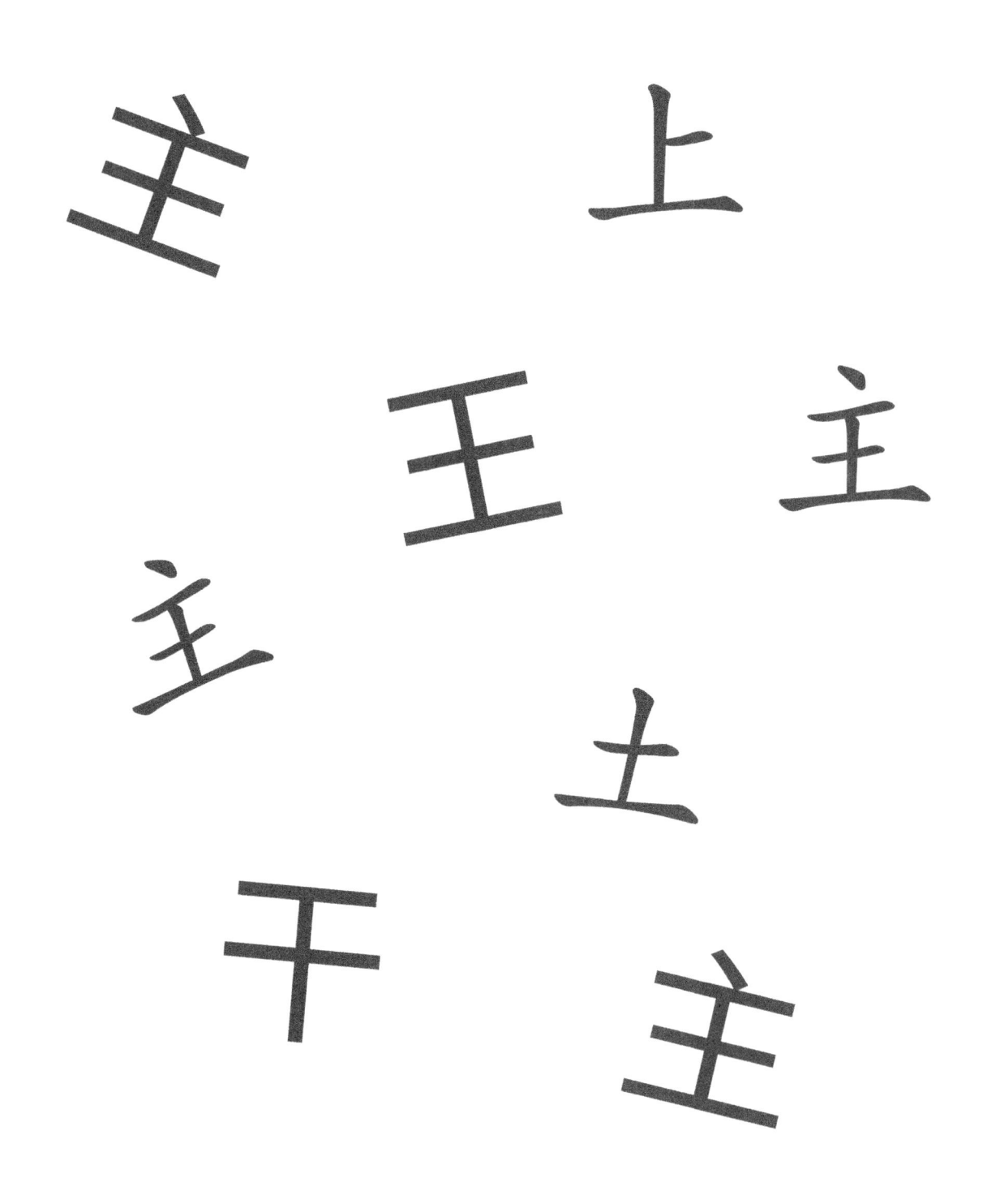

唸唸看
Read-Aloud

- 馬兒的主人買了新的馬車。
The horse's owner bought a new horse cart.

- 馬兒就可以拉很多東西了。
The horse can then pull a lot of things.

- 馬兒主要的工作是拉車。
The horse's main job is to pull the cart.

- 馬兒每天要走很長的山路。
The horse needs to travel a long mountain road everyday.

- 馬車上坐了一些人正在唱歌。
There are some people sitting on the cart singing.

恭喜你完成了這一課,請回到第一頁將本課的愛心塗上顏色。
Congratulations! You have completed a lesson. Please color the heart for this lesson on page 1.

第十二課

Lesson 12 Shí – real; true; honest; solid

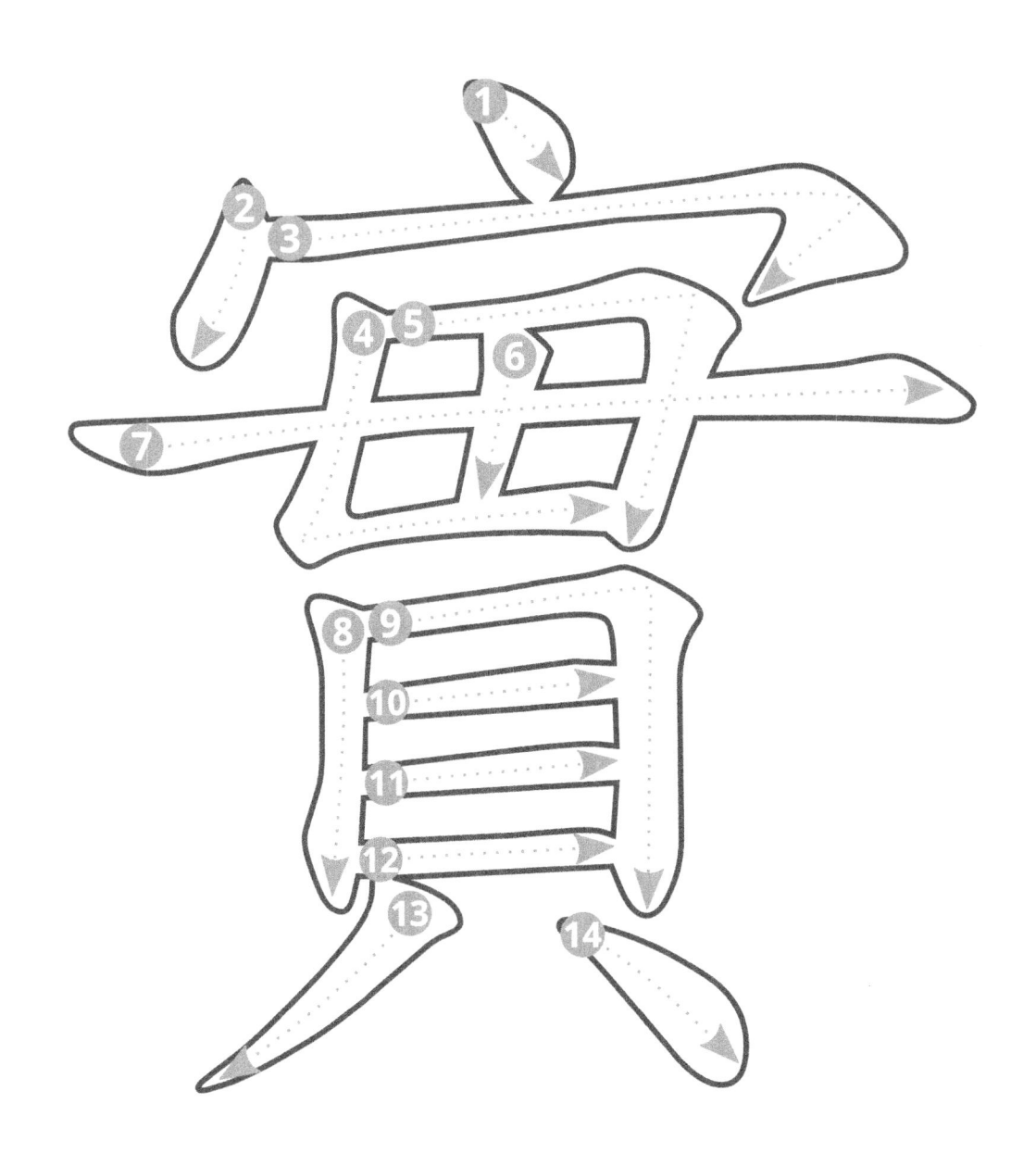

本書中的國字筆順是依據中華民國教育部「常用國字標準字體筆順學習網」的筆劃順序彙編。
The stroke orders of the characters in this workbook follow the stroke orders provided on the "Learning Program for Stroke Order of Frequently Used Chinese Characters" website of the Ministry of Education, R.O.C. (Taiwan).

47

將有「實」字的果實著色。
Color the acorns with the character 實.

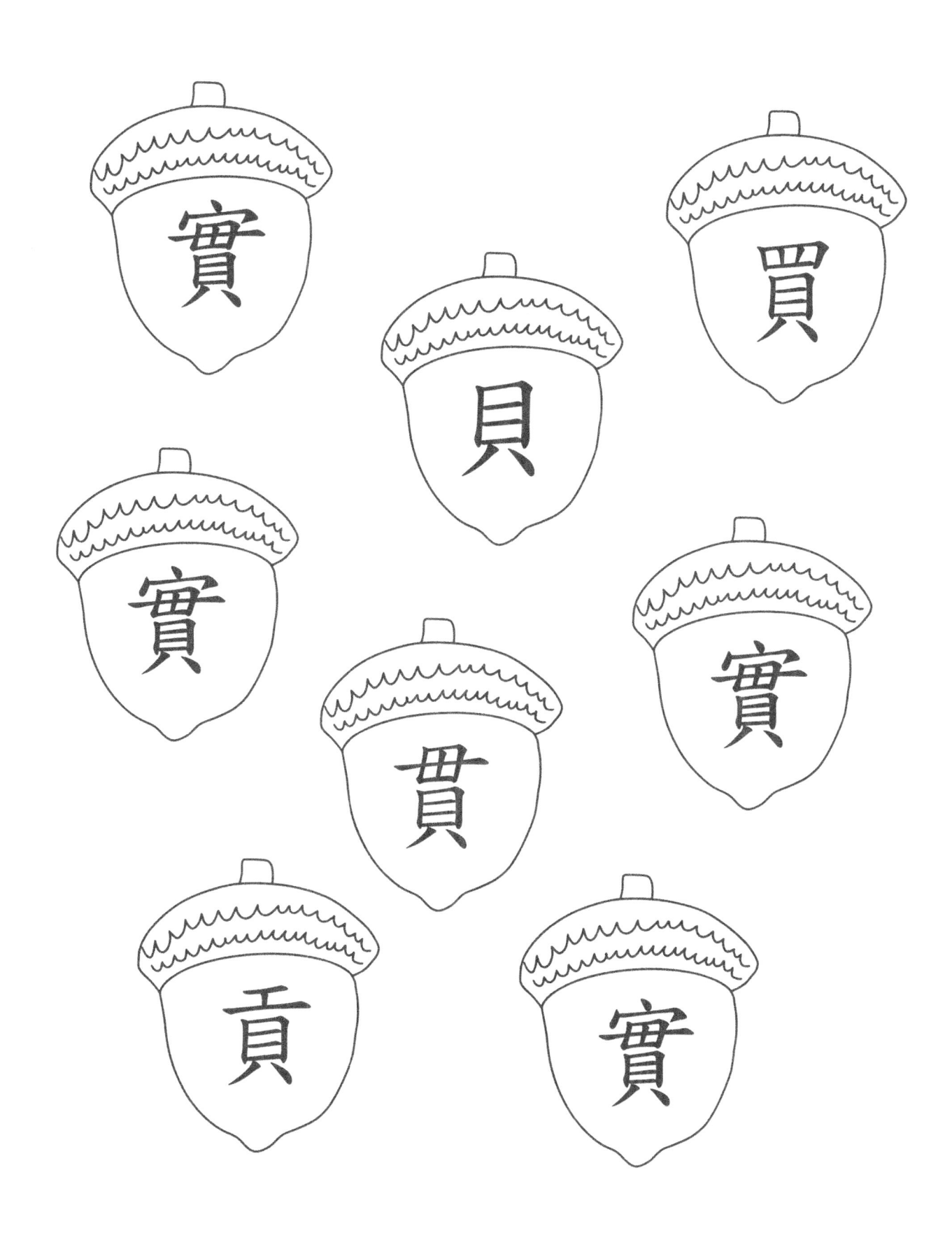

實　買　貝　實　貫　實　貢　實

請唸出路牌上的字。
Please read aloud all the signs on both sides of the road.

實話實說

實在

老實

唸唸看
Read-Aloud

- 小鳥早上先吃了家門口樹上的果實。

  In the morning, the little bird first ate the fruit on the tree in front of the house.

- 天黑時又喝了杯子裡的水。

  At night, (it) drank the water in the cup also.

- 媽媽馬上去外面買些新的水果。

  Mom immediately went out to buy some new fruit.

- 我想要小鳥的主人看好小鳥。

  I want the bird's owner to keep an eye on the little bird.

- 小鳥吃得實在太多了。

  The little bird really eats too much.

恭喜你完成了這一課，請回到第一頁將本課的愛心塗上顏色。
Congratulations! You have completed a lesson. Please color the heart for this lesson on page 1.

第十三課

Lesson 13 Yú – fish

本書中的國字筆順是依據中華民國教育部「常用國字標準字體筆順學習網」的筆劃順序彙編。
The stroke orders of the characters in this workbook follow the stroke orders provided on the "Learning Program for Stroke Order of Frequently Used Chinese Characters" website of the Ministry of Education, R.O.C. (Taiwan).

「魚」是象形字，它看起來就像一條魚的樣子。
The character 魚 is a pictograph. It looks like a fish.

連連看
Draw lines to the matching objects.

鳥 •

狗 •

魚 •

貓 •

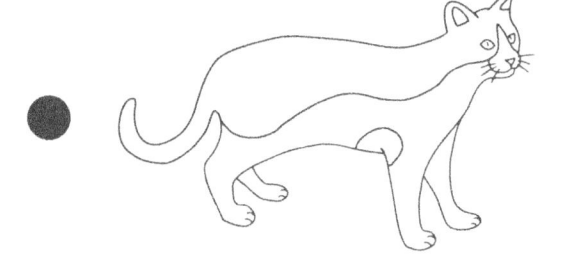

唸唸看
Read-Aloud

- 我最愛人魚公主的故事了。
  My favorite story is the story of The Little Mermaid.

- 這個故事我已經看過八次了。
  I read this story for eight times already.

- 人魚公主的歌聲實在太動聽了。
  The mermaid princess' voice is really touching.

- 妹妹問：「公主在水裡唱歌會不會喝到一些水。」
  (My) younger sister asked, "Will the princess drink in some water (when she) is singing in the water?"

- 我馬上跑去問媽媽。
  I immediately ran to ask Mom.

恭喜你完成了這一課，請回到第一頁將本課的愛心塗上顏色。
Congratulations! You have completed a lesson. Please color the heart for this lesson on page 1.

第十四課

Lesson 14 Dìng – to set; to fix

本書中的國字筆順是依據中華民國教育部「常用國字標準字體筆順學習網」的筆劃順序彙編。
The stroke orders of the characters in this workbook follow the stroke orders provided on the "Learning Program for Stroke Order of Frequently Used Chinese Characters" website of the Ministry of Education, R.O.C. (Taiwan).

跟著「定」字從 ➡ 到 ★ 走出迷宮。
Follow the characters 定 from the arrow to the star to exit the maze.

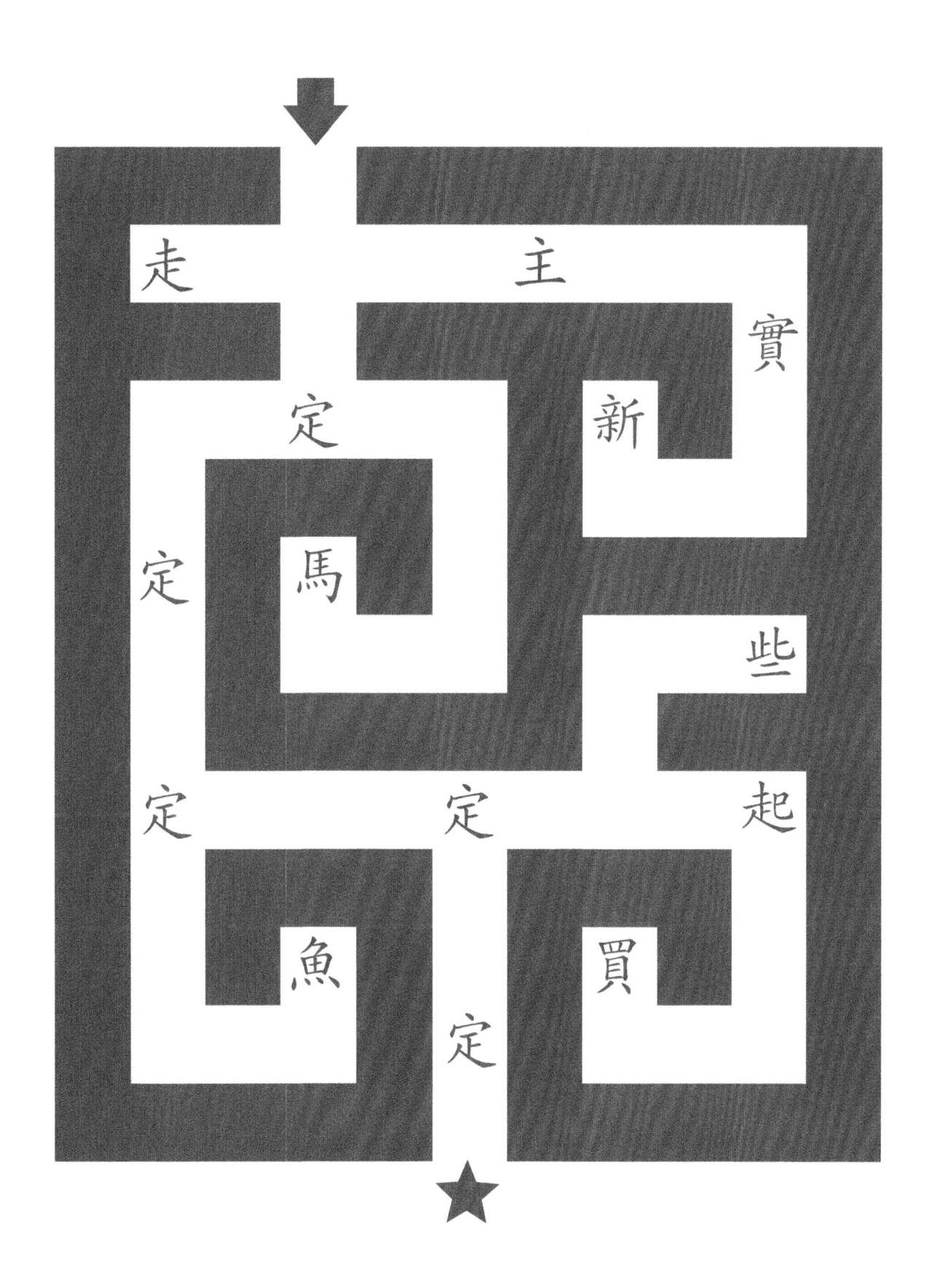

56

請將有「定」字的區塊上色。
Please color the area with the character 定.

唸唸看
Read-Aloud

- 馬兒愛吃草所以跑得快。
Horses love to eat grass and therefore can run fast.

- 貓兒愛吃魚所以跳得高。
Cats love to eat fish and therefore can jump high.

- 小鳥愛吃果實所以飛得快。
Little birds love to eat fruits and therefore can fly quickly.

- 公主一定是不吃點心所以長得美麗。
I'm sure that the princess is beautiful because (she) doesn't eat desserts.

- 我一定也要少吃點心。
I must also eat less desserts.

恭喜你完成了這一課,請回到第一頁將本課的愛心塗上顏色。
Congratulations! You have completed a lesson. Please color the heart for this lesson on page 1.

58

第十五課

Lesson 15 Wáng – king or monarch; best or strongest of its type

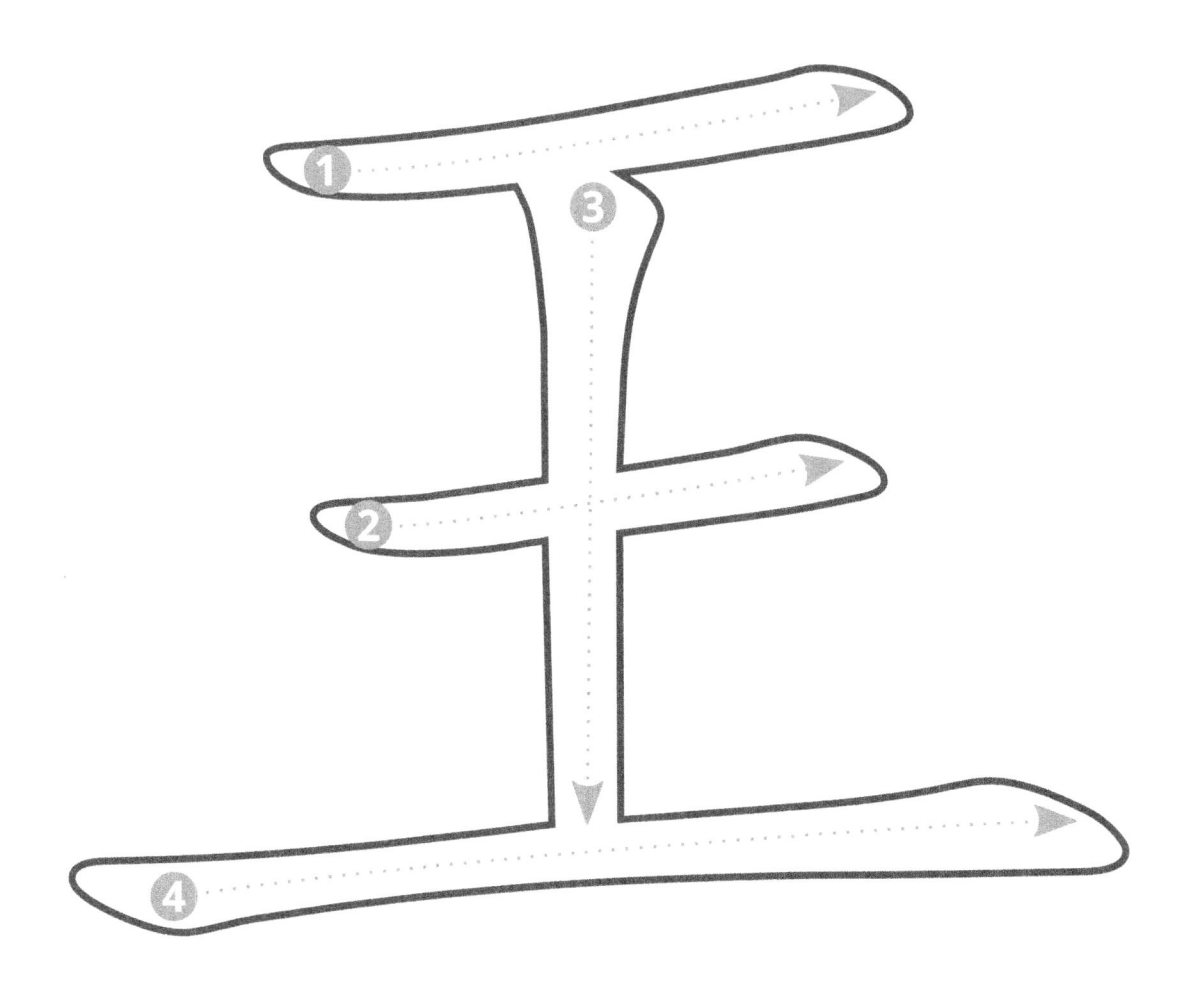

本書中的國字筆順是依據中華民國教育部「常用國字標準字體筆順學習網」的筆劃順序彙編。
The stroke orders of the characters in this workbook follow the stroke orders provided on the "Learning Program for Stroke Order of Frequently Used Chinese Characters" website of the Ministry of Education, R.O.C. (Taiwan).

圖案中有的東西在（ ）中打勾。
Put a check next to the items that are in the picture.

（ ） 白雲　（ ） 國王　（ ） 狗
（ ） 王子　（ ） 天空　（ ） 馬
（ ） 馬車　（ ） 公主　（ ） 書

60

請將皇冠著色並找出到達「王」字的路。
Please color the crown and find the path leading to the character 王.

請將皇冠著色並找出到達「王」字的路。
Please color the crown and find the path leading to the character 王.

唸唸看
Read-Aloud

- 人魚公主的故事實在太好看了。
  The Little Mermaid's story is really good.

- 你一定也會想看的。
  I'm sure you will want to read it too.

- 故事裡有國王、王子和公主。
  There is a king, prince, and a princess in the story.

- 王子愛聽好聽的音樂。
  The prince loves to listen to good music.

- 可是公主失去了美麗的歌聲。
  But the princess lost her beautiful voice.

恭喜你完成了這一課,請回到第一頁將本課的愛心塗上顏色。
Congratulations! You have completed a lesson. Please color the heart for this lesson on page 1.

第十六課

Lesson 16 Wù – thing; object; matter

本書中的國字筆順是依據中華民國教育部「常用國字標準字體筆順學習網」的筆劃順序彙編。
The stroke orders of the characters in this workbook follow the stroke orders provided on the "Learning Program for Stroke Order of Frequently Used Chinese Characters" website of the Ministry of Education, R.O.C. (Taiwan).

請圈出所有的動物並唸出下方的文字。
Please circle all the animals and read aloud the characters at the bottom.

動物園裡有好多
可愛的動物

請圈出與圖案相對應的句子。
Please circle the phrase that best describes the picture.

這些動物在動物園看的到。
動物們正在喝水。
這些動物裡面有牛和羊。

唸唸看
Read-Aloud

- 故事裡的王子們當然都愛動物。
  Princes in stories must all love animals.

- 白馬王子一定愛馬兒。
  Prince Charming must love horses.

- 人魚公主裡的王子一定愛魚。
  The prince in The Little Mermaid must love fish.

- 馬和魚全都是動物。
  Horses and fish are both animals.

- 動物實在是太可愛了。
  Animals are really so cute.

恭喜你完成了這一課，請回到第一頁將本課的愛心塗上顏色。
Congratulations! You have completed a lesson. Please color the heart for this lesson on page 1.

第十七課

Lesson 17 Guài – odd; strange; monster; to blame

本書中的國字筆順是依據中華民國教育部「常用國字標準字體筆順學習網」的筆劃順序彙編。
The stroke orders of the characters in this workbook follow the stroke orders provided on the "Learning Program for Stroke Order of Frequently Used Chinese Characters" website of the Ministry of Education, R.O.C. (Taiwan).

請圈出所有的怪物並唸出下方的文字。
Please circle all the monsters and read aloud the characters at the bottom.

怪物好可怕

請圈出與圖案相對應的句子。
Please circle the phrase that best describes the picture.

這個怪物有四隻手。
怪物正在聽音樂。
這是一個綠色的怪物。

唸唸看
Read-Aloud

- 從前有一隻怪物，樣子很可怕。
  In the past, there is a scary looking monster.

- 他有七隻手，六隻耳朵和五個頭。
  It has seven hands, six ears, and five heads.

- 這隻怪物常常吃魚。
  The monster often eats fish.

- 我想人魚公主一定會很怕他。
  I think the mermaid princess will definitely be afraid of it.

- 王子一定不會怕怪物的。
  The prince will definitely not be afraid of the monster.

恭喜你完成了這一課，請回到第一頁將本課的愛心塗上顏色。
Congratulations! You have completed a lesson. Please color the heart for this lesson on page 1.

第十八課

Lesson 18 Shí – to eat; food

本書中的國字筆順是依據中華民國教育部「常用國字標準字體筆順學習網」的筆劃順序彙編。
The stroke orders of the characters in this workbook follow the stroke orders provided on the "Learning Program for Stroke Order of Frequently Used Chinese Characters" website of the Ministry of Education, R.O.C. (Taiwan).

連連看
Connect the phrases to the correct pictures.

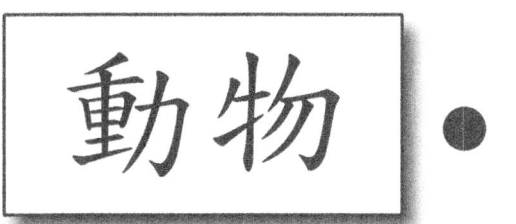

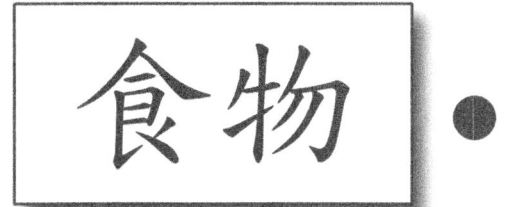

動物 ●

食物 ●

怪物 ●

71

請將三個相同的物品連成一線。
Please connect the same items to win the tic-tac-toe.

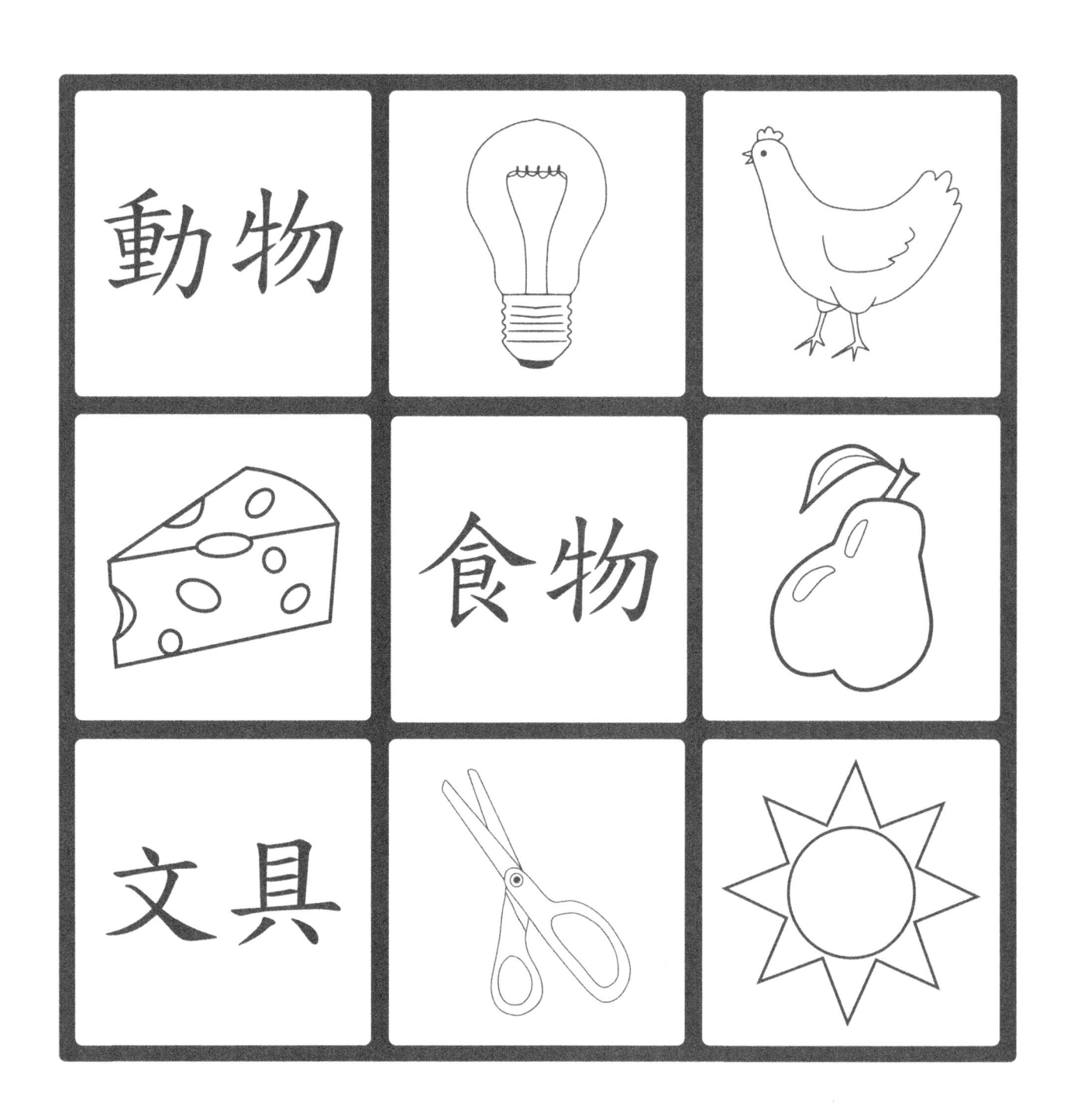

動物	(燈泡)	(雞)
(芝士)	食物	(梨)
文具	(剪刀)	(太陽)

唸唸看
Read-Aloud

- 有一天王國裡發生了很怪的事。
  One day, a strange thing happened in the kingdom.

- 天空中出現了十個太陽。
  Ten suns appeared in the sky.

- 人們都沒有水和食物了。
  The people don't have water and food.

- 後來九個太陽不見了。
  And then nine of the suns disappeared.

- 大家又有食物和水了。
  Everybody had food and water again.

恭喜你完成了這一課，請回到第一頁將本課的愛心塗上顏色。
Congratulations! You have completed a lesson. Please color the heart for this lesson on page 1.

第十九課

Lesson 19 Shuì – to sleep

本書中的國字筆順是依據中華民國教育部「常用國字標準字體筆順學習網」的筆劃順序彙編。
The stroke orders of the characters in this workbook follow the stroke orders provided on the "Learning Program for Stroke Order of Frequently Used Chinese Characters" website of the Ministry of Education, R.O.C. (Taiwan).

請將下方的字格剪下來讓孩子選擇正確的字貼上。
Please cut out the characters at the bottom and paste the correct one.

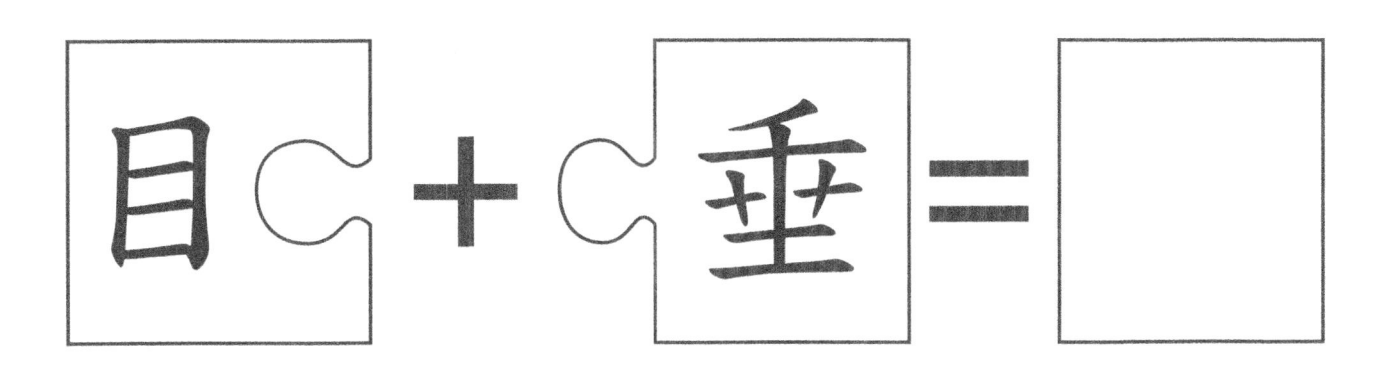

75

目 + 垂 = ☐

| 睡 | 垂 | 倕 | 諈 | 捶 |

跟著「睡」字從 ➡ 到 ★ 走出迷宮。
Follow the characters 睡 from the arrow to the star to exit the maze.

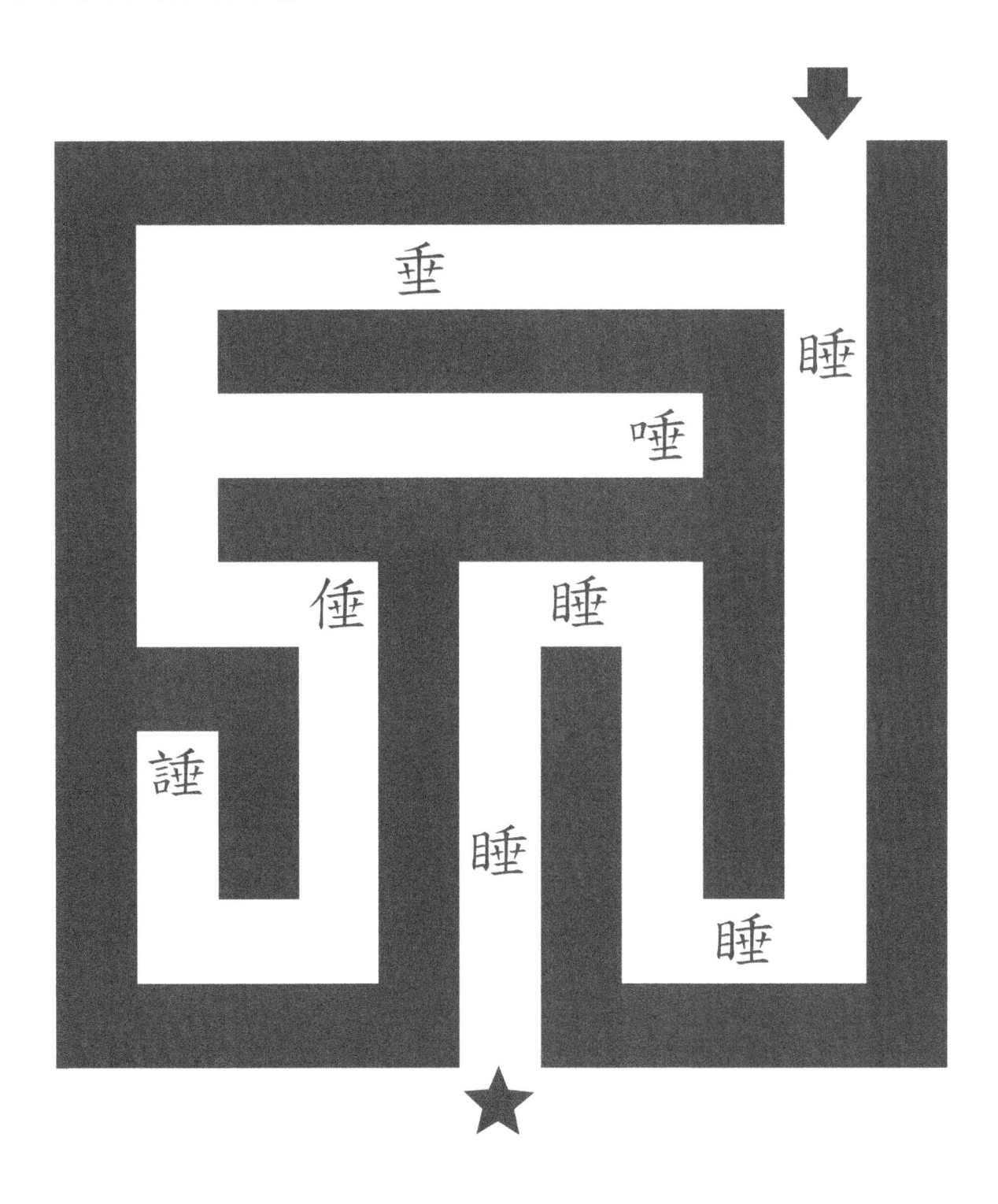

唸唸看
Read-Aloud

- 有一天王子不小心走到怪物家裡。

  One day, the prince accidentally entered the monster's home.

- 怪物吃完食物後就睡了。

  The monster fell asleep after eating.

- 還好怪物睡著了。

  Good thing that the monster was asleep.

- 王子才能回到家。

  Therefore the prince could return home.

- 等到天亮怪物起來就不好了。

  (If he) waited until the monster woke up in the morning, (it) will be bad.

恭喜你完成了這一課,請回到第一頁將本課的愛心塗上顏色。
Congratulations! You have completed a lesson. Please color the heart for this lesson on page 1.

第二十課

Lesson 20 Jiào – a sleep; a nap
Jué – to feel; thinking

本書中的國字筆順是依據中華民國教育部「常用國字標準字體筆順學習網」的筆劃順序彙編。
The stroke orders of the characters in this workbook follow the stroke orders provided on the "Learning Program for Stroke Order of Frequently Used Chinese Characters" website of the Ministry of Education, R.O.C. (Taiwan).

找到「覺」字圈出來。
Find the characters 覺 and circle them.

見

覺　　　　　　　覺

　　怪

　　學

學　　　　　覺

　　睡　　　物

將點心塗色並唸出下方的文字。
Color the desserts and read aloud the characters at the bottom.

我覺得點心好好吃

唸唸看
Read-Aloud

- 怪物睡覺前要吃很多食物。
  The monster needs to eat lots of food before sleeping.

- 他的食物就是人。
  It's food is people.

- 我覺得怪物很可怕。
  I think the monster is very scary.

- 如果沒吃人他就會大叫。
  If it doesn't eat people, it will shout.

- 吃完一個人還想再吃一個人。
  After it finishes eating one person it will still want to eat another.

恭喜你完成了這一課,請回到第一頁將本課的愛心塗上顏色。
Congratulations! You have completed a lesson. Please color the heart for this lesson on page 1.

第二十一課

Lesson 21 Chuáng – bed

本書中的國字筆順是依據中華民國教育部「常用國字標準字體筆順學習網」的筆劃順序彙編。
The stroke orders of the characters in this workbook follow the stroke orders provided on the "Learning Program for Stroke Order of Frequently Used Chinese Characters" website of the Ministry of Education, R.O.C. (Taiwan).

請圈出所有床的圖案並唸出下方的文字。
Please circle all the beds and read aloud the characters at the bottom.

床是用來睡覺的

請圈出與圖案相對應的句子。
Please circle the phrase that best describes the picture.

天亮了,起床了。

給我一杯水喝。

今天的功課好多。

唸唸看
Read-Aloud

- 妹妹睡覺前吃了怪怪的食物，所以睡不著。

(My) younger sister ate some weird food before sleeping, therefore, she could not fall asleep.

- 她自己一個人坐在床邊唱了三首歌。

She sat alone on the side of the bed and sang three songs.

- 當她唱到第四首時，就受不了了。

When she reached the fourth song, (she) could not stand it anymore.

- 然後她就在床上睡著了。

Then, she fell asleep on the bed.

恭喜你完成了這一課，請回到第一頁將本課的愛心塗上顏色。
Congratulations! You have completed a lesson. Please color the heart for this lesson on page 1.

第二十二課

Lesson 22 Tǎng – to recline; to lie down

請圈出與圖案相對應的句子。
Please circle the phrase that best describes the picture.

太陽出來了。

弟弟正在看書。

他躺在床上睡著了。

88

連連看
Draw lines to the matching pictures.

躺 •

跳 •

飛 •

跑 •

唸唸看
Read-Aloud

- 灰色的天空下起了大雨。
  The gray sky started to rain heavily.

- 下雨的日子很好睡覺。
  It is easy to sleep on rainy days.

- 我在床上躺了一會兒。
  I laid on the bed for a little.

- 躺著躺著就睡著了。
  I fell asleep (while) lying there.

- 起床後想吃好吃的食物。
  After I got up, (I) wanted to eat delicious food.

恭喜你完成了這一課,請回到第一頁將本課的愛心塗上顏色。
Congratulations! You have completed a lesson. Please color the heart for this lesson on page 1.

第二十三課

Lesson 23 Mèng – dream

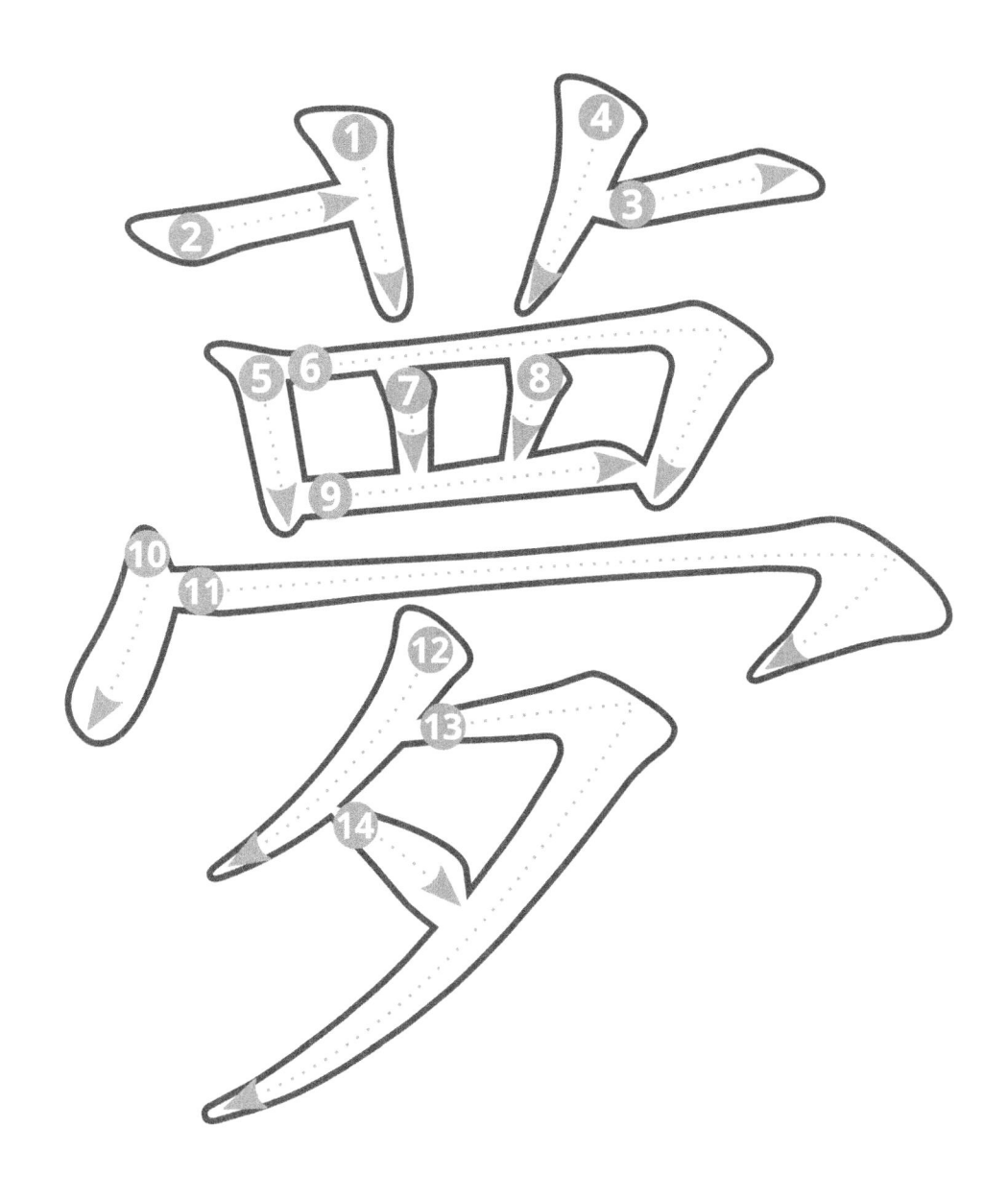

本書中的國字筆順是依據中華民國教育部「常用國字標準字體筆順學習網」的筆劃順序彙編。
The stroke orders of the characters in this workbook follow the stroke orders provided on the "Learning Program for Stroke Order of Frequently Used Chinese Characters" website of the Ministry of Education, R.O.C. (Taiwan).

請在下方的框中畫上一條魚並唸出下方的文字。
Please draw a fish in the bubble and read aloud the characters at the bottom.

小花貓夢到魚

請跟著慢跑的先生穿過公園並唸出路牌上的文字。
Read aloud the signs as the man runs through the park.

作夢

夢想

美夢

唸唸看
Read-Aloud

- 我躺在床上睡覺時做了一個夢。
  When I was lying on the bed sleeping, I had a dream.

- 我夢到老師正在教我寫字。
  I dreamed that the teacher was teaching me how to write.

- 這是我這個月第二次做同樣的夢。
  This is the second time this month that I had the same dream.

- 因為我愛學寫字。
  This is because I love learning to write.

- 所以才會不停地做同樣的夢。
  Therefore, I keep on having the same dream non-stop.

恭喜你完成了這一課,請回到第一頁將本課的愛心塗上顏色。
Congratulations! You have completed a lesson. Please color the heart for this lesson on page 1.

第二十四課

Lesson 24 Biàn – to change; to become different; to transform

本書中的國字筆順是依據中華民國教育部「常用國字標準字體筆順學習網」的筆劃順序彙編。
The stroke orders of the characters in this workbook follow the stroke orders provided on the "Learning Program for Stroke Order of Frequently Used Chinese Characters" website of the Ministry of Education, R.O.C. (Taiwan).

請將三個相同的字連成一線。
Please connect the same characters to win the tic-tac-toe.

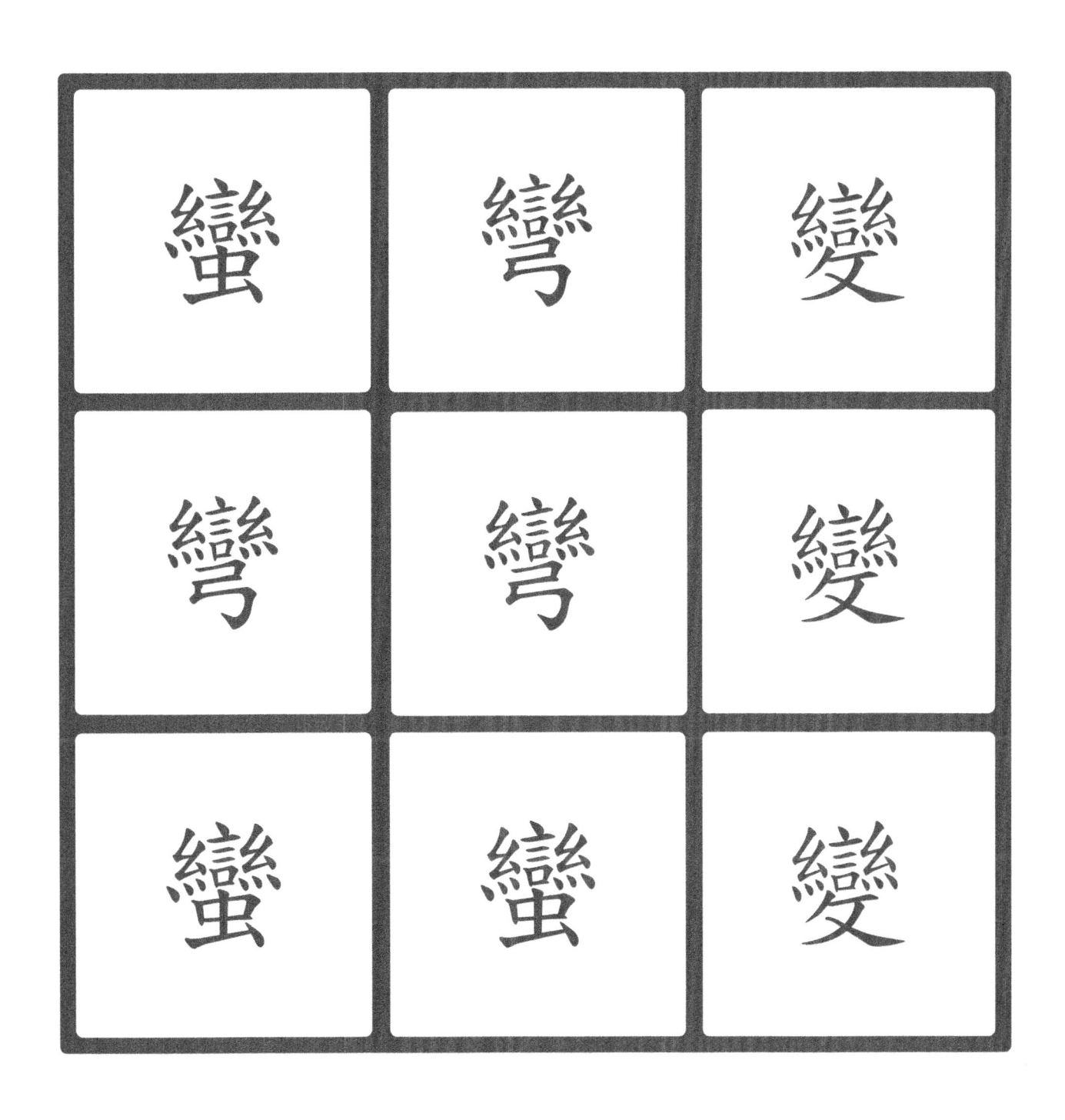

蠻	彎	變
彎	彎	變
蠻	蠻	變

請圈出與圖案相對應的句子。
Please circle the phrase that best describes the picture.

變出一隻兔子。

變出了一隻貓。

兔子不見了。

唸唸看
Read-Aloud

- 我躺在床上睡覺時做了一個夢。
  When I was lying on the bed sleeping, I had a dream.

- 我夢到我把弟弟變不見了。
  I dreamed that I made (my) younger brother disappeared.

- 然後我變得很大。
  And then I became really huge.

- 真是一個可怕的夢。
  What a scary dream.

恭喜你完成了這一課，請回到第一頁將本課的愛心塗上顏色。
Congratulations! You have completed a lesson. Please color the heart for this lesson on page 1.

第二十五課

Lesson 25 Chéng – to succeed; to complete; to become

本書中的國字筆順是依據中華民國教育部「常用國字標準字體筆順學習網」的筆劃順序彙編。
The stroke orders of the characters in this workbook follow the stroke orders provided on the "Learning Program for Stroke Order of Frequently Used Chinese Characters" website of the Ministry of Education, R.O.C. (Taiwan).

請唸出河邊牌子上的文字。
Read aloud the signs on the river banks.

變成

成功

長大成人

成年

100

跟著「成」字從 ➡ 到 ★ 走出迷宮。
Follow the characters 成 from the arrow to the star to exit the maze.

唸唸看
Read-Aloud

- 我做了一個夢。
  I had a dream.

- 我夢到我躺在地上。
  I dreamed that I was lying on the ground.

- 我的床變成了一個怪物。
  My bed turned into a monster.

- 我變成了一頭牛。
  I turned into a cow.

- 這個夢好怪。
  This dream is weird.

恭喜你完成了這一課，請回到第一頁將本課的愛心塗上顏色。
Congratulations! You have completed a lesson. Please color the heart for this lesson on page 1.

獎狀
Certificate of Achievement

恭喜

Congratulations to

完成趣味識字第十冊。
特發此狀以資鼓勵！

for completing Fun with Chinese Workbook 10.

簽名 Signature

日期 Date

Made in the USA
Las Vegas, NV
01 May 2025